SOUTH DOWNS

WALKS

Ben Perkins

30 Walks with sketch maps

COUNTRYSIDE BOOKS
NEWBURY, BERKSHIRE

*Countryside Books' walking guides cover most areas of England
and include the following series:*

*County Rambles
Walks For Motorists
Exploring Long Distance Paths
Literary Walks
Pub Walks*

A complete list is available from the publishers.

First published by Frederick Warne Ltd
This edition published 1993
© Ben Perkins 1993

All rights reserved.
No reproduction permitted without
the prior permission of the publishers:

COUNTRYSIDE BOOKS
3 Catherine Road
Newbury, Berkshire

ISBN 1 85306 217 0

Sketch maps by Chartwell Illustrators

Cover photograph taken by Andy Williams

Publishers' Note
At the time of publication all rights of way were shown on the definitive
maps maintained by local councils or were well-established permitted
routes, but it should be borne in mind that diversion orders may be
made from time to time and permissions may be withdrawn.

Produced through MRM Associates Ltd., Reading
Printed in England by J. W. Arrowsmith Ltd., Bristol

Contents

Introduction

The thirty walks in this book are spread out over the entire length of the South Downs in East and West Sussex, from Butser Hill just over the Hampshire border (Walk 1) to the hills above Eastbourne (Walk 30). They are fairly evenly distributed though there may be a slight bias in favour of the more extensively wooded downland in West Sussex.

As a rough guide, the following centres might provide a suitable base for the walks indicated.

Chichester	Walks 1–8
Arundel	Walks 9–14
Worthing	Walks 15–18
Brighton	Walks 19–23
Lewes	Walks 24–26
Seaford or Eastbourne	Walks 27–30

The individual walks vary in length between 3½ and 9 miles. They are all circular, starting and finishing at points where there should normally be ample parking space available. For leisurely walking, allow 2 miles an hour plus time for stops. I have not specifically mentioned refreshment facilities in the descriptions, but pubs on the routes are marked on the sketch maps.

For more energetic ramblers who might prefer a longer walk, I have designed a number of the circuits so that they can be linked together in pairs, using one starting point. The link points and routes are indicated in the text and on the sketch maps.

Walk 4 may be linked with Walks 5 and/or 6 to give a total distance of 10½, 12 or 17½ miles.

Walks 8 and 10 can be joined together, providing a total length of 15¼ miles.

Walks 9 and 10 combine to give a fairly strenuous 18-mile circuit.

Walks 11 and 12 may be linked to give a total of 11 miles.

Walks 14 and 15 together make 13½ miles.

Walks 16 and 19 combine to give 12½ miles.

Walks 25 and 26 together give a 13-mile trek.

Walks 27 and 30 together make 12½ miles.

Walks 28 and 29 make 11½ miles through the Heritage Coast area.

Although it should be possible to complete the walks using only the route descriptions and the sketch maps, I certainly would not recommend attempting them without an Ordnance Survey map. The sketch maps are not to scale and provide, in any case, a guide only to features actually on the route of the walk. For rambling in the relatively uncluttered downland landscape the 1:50,000 scale OS maps are generally quite adequate and the latest editions indicate rights of way in red. To cover all the walks in the book you will need three sheets,

Numbers 197, 198 and 199, and before each walk I have indicated which particular map will be required. An OS map will enable you to find your way to the starting points of the walks, for which I have included a grid reference in each case. It will also allow you to put the walk in the context of the surrounding countryside and to pick out more distant features not shown on the sketch map. It might also be most valuable if you do happen, in error, to wander off the described route or choose to modify or extend a particular walk.

A word about signposting and maintenance of paths. In West Sussex you will find that many of the paths have been waymarked with wooden signposts. These are easily vandalized, however, and have a habit of disappearing. I have, therefore, deliberately omitted almost all reference to them in the written walk descriptions. Over the last few years the county councils of East and West Sussex have put a good deal more effort into the maintenance of public paths than previously. In the downland area, where most of the rights of way are well established and regularly used, there are now no serious obstructions. Regrettably, the ploughing out of public paths still occurs in spite of the 1990 Act, which strengthened the law restricting this tiresome practice.

All the walks follow public rights of way or paths where public access is permitted or recognized (often on National Trust land). Occasionally, where a path has been obstructed on its true line I have had to deviate a little but whenever this has been necessary I have indicated it in the route description.

If you enjoy the walks in this book and would like to help combat the frequent threats of encroachment on to the Downs by trunk road and urban development, you might consider joining the Society of Sussex Downsmen. Founded in 1923, the Society's main objects are the conservation of the South Downs and the encouragement of their use for quiet recreation. More information about the Society's work and membership application forms may be obtained from the Secretary at 93 Church Road, Hove BN3 2BA, East Sussex.

In the preparation of this book, I am glad to acknowledge the help of my father, Denis Perkins. He has provided much of the background information included with the walks. It was he who introduced me to the pleasures of downland walking at an early age, and I am delighted he has agreed to write the introductory article on the South Downs which follows.

Ben Perkins

KEY MAP (WEST)
Downland area shaded
Numbers indicate the start
of the walks

10 miles (approx.)
(not to scale)

10 kilometres (approx.)

KEY MAP (EAST)
Downland area shaded
Numbers indicate the start
of the walks

THE SOUTH DOWNS

The South Downs stretch for eighty miles, from Butser Hill in Hampshire, which is over twelve miles inland to Beachy Head, where they rise up out of the sea. These 'blunt, bowheaded, whalebacked Downs', as Kipling called them, are visible from almost everywhere in Sussex. They are your southern horizon, whenever you see them from the Weald — a gently undulating skyline, ragged with woodland in the western half of the county, smooth and clean-cut in the eastern half, where the sea lies hidden only a few miles beyond. They are a modest range of hills, only 813 feet high at Ditchling Beacon and 836 at Tegleaze Hill, the highest points in East and West Sussex, but strangely impressive as you approach their steep northern escarpment, almost cliff-like in places. It is fascinating to see how the hillshapes and their relationship to one another change as you cross the Weald, outlying headlands like Wolstonbury and Mount Caburn alternately merging with the rest of the Downs or standing clearly detached.

These Downs are solid chalk, a limestone which is the result of billions of minute sea-shells living and dying beneath ancient seas. Both North and South Downs are the remains of an immense submarine dome of chalk which once covered the Weald to the height of possibly two or three thousand feet, with Ashdown Forest an island in the middle of the sea. To the layman, this is one of geology's more comprehensible theories. The Downs really do look as though this might have happened, and it is not too difficult to imagine how millions of years of erosion have left gaps through the hills which now connect Weald with coastal plain and sea. There are not many of them; four river valleys, carrying the Arun, Adur, Ouse and Cuckmere, and four dry valleys with main roads. A few other roads cross the Downs by climbing the escarpment diagonally in the manner of ancient trackways, which once perhaps they were. It is not much in eighty miles and partly explains why the Downs seem lonely and empty in spite of the proximity of the crowded coastal plain.

It is the chalk which gives the Downs their special character. Chalk is porous like a sponge and quickly absorbs the rainfall, which then breaks out in springs where the chalk meets sandstone or clay lower down. This can be seen at Fulking (Walk 20), where the water gushes out by the roadside, or at West Firle (Walk 25), where there is an old spring in the middle of the village. These are two of the spring-line villages strung out along the foot of the northern escarpment, often only a mile or so apart. There are also villages in the valleys, especially the river valleys, but very few on the hill-tops.

It is also partly the chalk which determines what will grow in the thin skin of soil which covers it. This soil is poor, dry and wind-swept and for centuries has been mostly grassland, mixed with an amazing variety of small low-growing plants, including cowslips in spring and the wild thyme which used to give the Downs their special summer smell. In autumn festoons of Old Man's Beard whiten patches of scrub or woodland. White is a characteristic feature of the downland landscape; white ploughed fields, old chalk pits, worn tracks climbing hillsides, chalk cliffs. And the flowers determine the birds and butterflies. There is an exquisite butterfly called the Chalkhill Blue. To the ordinary walker the most notable birds of the downland are the joyously-singing larks rising everywhere from grass or cornfield and the birds hovering in the updraught from the escarpment, especially when the wind is in the north, the seagulls, lapwings and occasional kestrels.

Until modern times, it was the chalk which determined the choice of building material in downland villages. Flints are plentiful in chalk. Brick, stone and timber being hard to come by, flint was used for church and cottage alike. The same grey flints thickly litter the arable fields surrounding the groups of flint buildings, which look a natural part of the landscape.

The Cuckmere is the only undeveloped river mouth in Sussex, but none of the rivers is very large and the downland stretch of the Arun is even more beautiful than the Cuckmere valley. These are the West Sussex Downs and thickly wooded. Near Arundel the beech hangers of Arundel Park fall almost vertically to the riverbank. There seems to be no simple explanation of why the Downs west of the Arun should be so different. There are isolated clumps of beech everywhere on the Downs, but to the west there are whole forests, both young and mature, as well as mixed woodland and more yews than anywhere else in the British Isles. The hills are not so steep but the woods are glorious all through the year and there is always a good chance of seeing a few fallow deer running across a forest ride.

It is thought that left alone the Downs everywhere would revert to woodland, but man has prevented this. The primitive agriculture of Neolithic man followed by the nibbling sheep of the medieval wool industry left the Downs looking as I can remember them when I was a boy — miles and miles of bare, sweet-smelling, short-cropped turf. It is probably significant that *dun* in Old English meant a hill, but by the Middle ages a *doun* meant a sheepwalk; and that the eastern end of the Downs was always more associated with sheep than the west. This might explain why there are more trees west of the Arun.

The sheep have almost disappeared and except on the steep slopes the downland turf has been replaced by vast arable fields. This is the result of economics, aided by modern farm machinery. Widespread ploughing began during the Second World War. It is a big change; and yet it is strange to look through a schoolboy collection of snapshots taken on the South Downs between Eastbourne and Seaford, dated August 1922, and see how much is unchanged. There was little traffic and the roads were rough and narrow and thick with crushed flint. The bus warned you of its approach by appearing in the distance as a tiny white cloud of dust. Friston Mill has gone and so has the team of black oxen ploughing on the hill above Exceat Farm. But the 'little, lost, Down churches' look much the same, and the ox-bow curves of the Cuckmere river, and the shape of Firle Beacon; and so is the pleasure of walking along the ancient ridgeway and looking out over what Kipling called 'the wooded, dim, blue goodness of the Weald'. Even the vast prairie fields have a certain beauty, changing through the year from chalky white to spring green and then to ripe gold. There are still plenty of tracks across the Downs and with very few exceptions these rights of way have been respected, far more so than inland.

The Downs remain miraculously unspoilt when you compare them with the ruined coastal plain nearby. They feel quite primeval in sea-fog or thunderstorm. Even after all these years it is a great joy and privilege to walk over them and I envy anyone who is about to do so for the first time.

Denis Perkins

QUEEN ELIZABETH COUNTRY PARK AND BUTSER HILL

WALK 1

★

4 miles (6.5 km)

OS Landranger sheet 197

The first walk in the book is not a typical one and lovers of solitude might well prefer to give it a miss, though it is surprising how quickly it is possible to get away from the crowds who flock to the country park, particularly in the summer months, but who, in general, do not stray far from the Park Centre.

I can strongly recommend it as a good family walk, however, with two climbs, but not too long and with plenty to divert the interest of flagging children. A country park leaflet (obtainable from the Park Centre) includes a map showing a number of alternative paths through the Queen Elizabeth Forest and over War Down which will enable you to vary and lengthen the route.

Butser Hill, at 888 feet, is higher than any point on the Sussex Downs. Its prominent radio station makes it a landmark for miles around. It was an Iron Age hill-fort and is now at weekends the scene of various sports and pastimes, including hang-gliding and grass-skiing. The views from the top are not as wide as you might expect because you are looking out on very hilly country, but the church of East Meon provides a prominent landmark to the north-west and the Isle of Wight is visible to the south.

Park at the Queen Elizabeth Country Park Centre car park which is situated to the east of the A3 road about 5 miles south-west of Petersfield (OS map ref. 718184). NB. There is a charge for car parking.

Start the walk by going under the A3 via an underpass. A few yards beyond the main road, turn left off the slip road and follow the way marked 'horse route' up over the shoulder of Butser Hill, aiming for the radio mast on the summit.

Bear round to the right of the radio station and from a triangulation point beyond, keep roughly northwards along the ridge of Ramsdean Down. Go over a stile and follow the right hand side of the hill gently downwards. Cross a stile in the fence line to the right and drop steeply down. Where the open downland narrows to a point near the bottom, go over a stile to the right of a water trough, descend a flight of steps, and go straight across a field and out through a gate on to an access track. Turn left on this track, follow it out to a road and turn right.

Follow this road for ²/₃ mile, use the slip road to pass under the new

10

A3 road and, after another 250 yards, go ahead into Greenway Lane. In about 200 yards, just before a bridge over the railway, turn right on a wide track between hedges. In another 200 yards, go over a stile by a gate and turn right, uphill, between low banks. After about 300 yards, go forward over a stile and, shortly, left over a second stile. Join a forestry track on a bend and bear right, uphill, soon veering left with a quarry on your right. Now follow this clear wide track up round the side of War Down, ignoring a signed footpath which forks left.

You are now within the afforested area of Queen Elizabeth Country Park and there are a number of paths back to the car park all of which are marked on the map obtainable at the Park Centre. The simplest route will be described here.

In about 2/3 mile, a few yards after a broad track comes in from the left, fork right slightly downhill. At an open green space where there is a choice of three paths ahead, take the right hand one uphill. Ignore all side tracks and, on meeting a metalled road, go straight across. Ignore the first crossing horse track and in about 250 yards double back to the left on a harder track. Follow this downhill to the car park.

WEST MARDEN AND STANSTED FOREST

WALK 2

★

5½ miles (9 km)

OS Landranger sheet 197

West Marden is the only one of the Mardens without a church. Although probably the largest of the four, it is little more than an attractive straggle of flint cottages tucked under a wooded hillside to the west of the Chichester to Petersfield road. It is the starting point for this easy walk across wooded downland almost to the Hampshire border.

Stansted Forest was recorded as woodland in 1271 and it certainly has a feeling of antiquity about it. It is mostly coppice but there are many fine mature trees, usually oak, but also beech and some massive yew trees, reminiscent of the older ones in Kingley Vale. You may see fallow deer crossing one of the grassy forest rides.

Park at West Marden on the B2146 Chichester-Petersfield road about 8 miles north-west of Chichester. The village is immediately to the west of the B road, the turn-off being signposted to Rowlands Castle and Forestside. There is limited parking on the grass verge of the B2146 immediately to the north of the village turning. Alternatively there is room to park in the village street (OS map ref. 772136). If there is any difficulty in parking at West Marden continue along the Rowlands Castle road for 1½ miles and take the second turning to the left at Forestside. There are various parking areas on the north-south road through Stansted Forest, the most convenient being a large area at OS map ref. 755111 where you can pick up the walk from point A on the sketch map and as indicated in the route description.

Start the walk by taking the Rowlands Castle road as it climbs out of the village. Immediately beyond the last house and garden on the left, go left over a stile and keep along the left hand edge of the first field with a garden on your left. Go through a gate and keep straight ahead across the next field, with a wooden fence on your right, to cross a stile at a corner of woodland. Follow a path, narrow at first, along the foot of the hanger within the edge of the woodland. In about ¼ mile leave the wood over a stile into a field. Now keep along the edge of the field with the woodland on your right and in about 100 yards re-enter the wood over a stile by a gate. Once again the path keeps within the wooded area running parallel to the edge. It is now a more substantial track with a barbed wire fence to the left and soon with open hillside rising to the right. In ¼ mile go straight across a narrow road and through a bridle gate to follow another woodland track. In 75 yards go over a driveway and take a track which traverses the side of Watergate Hanger, climbing gradually.

At the top of the hanger, go over a crossing track, and in a few yards you will come out into the open and can turn right at a Y-junction to pass a flint cottage on the right and follow a hard farm track. Ignore tracks to right and left and then skirt to the left of farm buildings before turning left at a T-junction on to a metalled drive. In 350 yards, after passing another flint cottage, bear right with the main metalled drive which passes through a larch plantation. At the point where the plantation gives way on the left to a garden surrounded by metal railings, turn right on a path through the plantation. Ignore a crossing track and leave the plantation over a stile.

Now keep along the right hand edge of a field with more mature conifers to the right. In about 150 yards, turn left through almost 90 degrees and go straight out across an open field aiming towards a stile which you will soon be able to see at the corner of a wood under a large beech tree. Go through this gate and follow a narrow path for about 30 yards before turning left on a wider track. In another 150 yards or so, double back to the left on a well ridden bridleway which soon leaves the wood and follows a broad field headland strip with woodland to the right.

After nearly ½ mile the track cuts through a corner of woodland. About 50 yards after entering the woodland turn right on a track which leads through Stansted Forest for ¼ mile to a road at point A on the sketch map. (Walkers who have used the alternative parking area should start the route description here.)

Turn right along the road and in ¼ mile turn left along a clear gravel track. Go straight over several crossing tracks and in 350 yards, at a meeting of five ways, take the 'third exit' (half right). In another 180 yards, at another point where five paths meet, go almost directly ahead. After 10 yards, turn left along a path which passes between a pit on the left and a large yew tree on the right and on through coppiced woodland. Go straight over a crossing track and descend to leave the forest over a stile.

Go slightly right over a field in a dip to cross a second stile and climb for a few yards to a crossing track where turn right. Follow this narrow path which soon passes a cottage garden on the left and becomes a wider track which passes an old and overgrown quarry and then a young plantation on the right. Follow this track out to the road at Forestside.

Turn left along the road passing a small church on the left, and in about 50 yards go right over a stile and follow a clear track through woodland. Ignore a swing gate on the left and follow a narrow track eastwards along the edge of woodland. In 200 yards go left over a stile and cross a field to joint a road through a kissing gate.

Turn left along the road for 15 yards before turning right on a headland track. In 250 yards go over a stile and turn right along a farm track. In another 30 yards keep straight on, ignoring a left turn. Follow this old lane for nearly ½ mile out to a road.

Turn left along the road and in 150 yards turn right (signposted Walderton). In a little over 250 yards turn left over a stile and follow the remains of a hedge line for 400 yards before entering woodland over a stile. Drop down through the woods and follow a path along the side of the hill with views of West Marden opening out through the trees to the right. Finally go over a stile and descend half left across a small paddock which leads you on to a road. Turn right for West Marden and the car.

HARTING DOWNS AND NORTH MARDEN

WALK 3

★

5½ miles (9 km)

OS Landranger sheet 197

This is a varied walk, only a mile or so from the Hampshire border. The early part follows the South Downs Way and looks out over the Rother valley to the sandstone country rising towards Blackdown. There is an Iron Age hill-fort on Beacon Hill. Turning south, the walk goes through some beautiful wooded country, gently undulating and often quite unlike the rest of the Downs.

North Marden is little more than an isolated cluster of church and farm buildings. The church is small and simple — a single room with a most unusual curved chancel wall.

Park at the National Trust car park and picnic area to the east of the B2141 South Harting to Chichester road on the top of Harting Downs (OS map ref. 790181).

Start off eastwards along the South Downs Way following the edge of the Downs escarpment. In about ⅔ mile, after dropping down into Bramshott Bottom with its solid carved oak waypost erected by the Society of Sussex Downsmen, go ahead, climbing steeply to the triangulation point on the top of Beacon Hill at 795 feet.

From this point, on a clear day, there are magnificent views across the Weald with Blackdown to the north and Leith Hill and the North Downs to the north-east. To the east, Ditchling Beacon, over 30 miles away, can be picked out if conditions are good, and westwards the ridge of the Downs rises to its highest point at Butser Hill (Walk 1).

After dropping into another dip, go straight ahead over the lower summit of Pen Hill. Continue with the South Downs Way down the other side and, on reaching a belt of trees, turn right. In 100 yards turn right again on a grassy track which crosses a large field. Follow this track which soon runs between fences. This was once a road from Elsted over the Downs to North Marden. In about ½ mile the path drops down into a valley. A few yards after a path comes in from the left, fork right on a clear track which climbs out of the right side of the valley. Follow this track along the top edge of woodland and then, about 200 yards after a track comes in from the right, turn right on a narrow enclosed path which leaves the main track as it turns away to the left. Your path now runs between hedges for just over ¼ mile out to the B2141 road at North Marden.

Turn right along the road and in a little more than 100 yards, turn left. In another 50 yards go right along the access track to North Marden church. After passing the church on your right, go ahead downhill keeping to the left of a line of trees. After crossing a stile at the bottom, go half left across a narrow field to another stile. Go ahead (westwards) on a headland path which keeps to the left of two fields and continues within a narrow belt of scrubby woodland. In almost ½ mile, after passing through the left hand end of a plantation of conifers, go over a stile into a field and turn right along the edge of it with woodland to the right, your route being marked by a succession of stiles. After nearly ½ mile join a bridleway coming in from the left and follow it out to the main B2141 road, keeping to the right of a brick lodge and gateway.

This gateway is a back entrance to the Uppark estate, one of the largest in Sussex. There are, unfortunately, no rights of way across the park although some link paths are badly needed. The mansion, built in 1690 in elegant red brick and stone, has much of its original 18th century furnishings. It is now in National Trust ownership and was, at the time of writing, under repair following a disastrous fire.

For the walker, on reaching the B2141 road, there are more

16

immediate problems of access. Both West Sussex County Council and the landowner have promised a right of way on the opposite side of the road running parallel to it within the woodland. At the time of writing, however, this path has not materialized, and it is therefore necessary to turn left and walk along approximately 350 yards of dangerous road, after which you can turn right on a clear woodland track. About 250 yards along this track, turn left in line with a solitary conifer in the field to your right. Your path meanders through woodland at first and then follows along the left hand edge of an area of rough grassland for ½ mile. Towards the top of the hill turn left on a rutted track into woodland which will take you back to the car park.

CHILGROVE AND BOW HILL

WALK 4

★

4 miles (6.5 km)

OS Landranger sheet 197

Chilgrove is a delightful spot, consisting of little more than an inn and a few cottages tucked down in a valley and immaculately set beside a green open space.

The short but beautiful walk climbs up from Chilgrove and follows a ridgeway track leading to fine open views from Bow Hill above Kingley Vale. The return route descends over Stoughton Down before climbing back over Chilgrove Hill.

Notes on Bow Hill and Kingley Vale are included under Walk 6. Walks 4 and 6 can be combined to form a total circuit of 9½ miles. The link point is indicated in the route description and on the sketch maps.

For the very energetic a link with Walk 5 is also indicated in the text and on the sketch map. When surveying the paths for inclusion in this book I walked all three on a crisp and sunny day in early April and I cannot recall a finer or more varied downland walk — 16 miles in all.

Park beside the green open space opposite the White Horse Inn at Chilgrove on the B2141 Chichester to South Harting road about 7 miles north of Chichester (OS map ref. 828145).

From the green, cross the B2141 road and follow a flint track up the flank of Chilgrove Hill. Keep to the main track until it levels out at the top of the hill. Here, fork left and follow a rutted track into woodland. In ¾ mile, after passing an isolated cottage on the right, ignore a left fork unless you would like to seek out Goosehill Camp down the hill to the left. It is a circular Iron Age earthwork enclosing half an acre but largely buried in a forest of yews. In its heyday it was possibly a fortified cattle enclosure.

To continue the walk, keep ahead along the ridge of the hill soon reaching a broad forest ride. In about ½ mile fine views open out on the left. Where the path broadens out on to an area of sloping grass downland, keep right (almost straight on) and in about 200 yards at a Kingley Vale Nature Reserve notice and map (the link point with Walk 6) turn back sharply to the right.

In just under 300 yards ignore a bridleway to the left and go ahead between gate posts and downhill over Stoughton Down, with a plantation of young conifers to your left. After about ¼ mile, join a roughly metalled track. Very shortly you will come to a meeting of six

White Horse P.H.
B2141 To South Harting
Start Park Here
B2141 To Chichester

N

WALK 4

Goosehill Camp

To Walk 5

Stoughton Down

Kingley Vale Nature
Reserve Notice

Bow Hill
Walk 6

ways, with a choice of two tracks almost directly ahead. Take the lower one on the left which drops downhill through a beech plantation. In about ½ mile join a roughly metalled track coming in from the right, and in another 300 yards, double sharply back to the right on a broad grassy track. (To link with Walk 5 keep straight on at this point on the hard track for 450 yards.)

Follow the grassy track and after a little over ¼ mile, ignore two right forks, go ahead through a gate and continue up the valley with a line of ancient beeches marking a parish boundary on the left. In ½ mile rejoin your outgoing route and keep straight ahead downhill into Chilgrove.

UP MARDEN AND STOUGHTON

WALK 5

★

7 miles (11 km)

OS Landranger sheet 197

An up-and-down walk through a wide variety of woodland scenery — not only young plantations of beech but several stretches of mixed woodland, some coppiced, some left wild and overgrown. A link with Walk 4 is indicated in the text and on the sketch map.

Up Marden is a tiny and remote hamlet high up in the Downs, little more than a farm and church adjoining.

Stoughton is an attractive village with a pub in a valley running down towards the Hampshire border.

East Marden is a compact flint and tile village in a hollow, with a characteristic little downland church and a village pump with a round thatched roof. It is not quite on the described walk but, allowing an extra mile, is well worth a short detour, either by footpath or along the road, both of which are indicated on the sketch map.

Park at the Stoughton Down Forestry Commission car parking area. This can be reached by turning right (eastwards) off the B2146 Chichester to Petersfield road at Walderton, about 7 miles north-west of Chichester. In 1 mile go through Stoughton and the car park is on the right, on a corner, about 1¼ miles further on up the valley (OS map ref. 815127).

On leaving the car park, turn right along the road. In about 300 yards, opposite a Forestry Commission notice 'Wildham Wood', turn left along an access drive, pass to the right of a house and climb within the left hand edge of woodland. Ignore all side turnings and climb through mature beeches at first and then on through a younger beech plantation. On leaving the wood, immediately turn right along the edge of it with a field on your left. At the end of the field, go straight ahead into woods again and descend to a road. (To visit East Marden take the field path which starts from this point as indicated on the sketch map.)

To continue the described walk turn left along the road for ¼ mile and then, about 50 yards before the road passes under power lines, turn left on a track into woods. Follow this track along the foot of the slope within the edge of the wood for another ¼ mile and then, at an oblique crossing track, turn left, steeply uphill. At the top of the wood keep straight ahead along the left hand edge of a field to join a road. Turn left along the road for 100 yards before turning right on a farm track. Access to Up Marden church is obtained from this track on the left. The 13th century church of St. Michael, Up Marden, is small, simple and candle-lit, with white walls and a brick floor. The wooden bell turret can no longer bear the weight of the three 17th century bells. Two of them stand on the chancel floor and the third has been hung by the porch outside.

Continue along the farm track and about 80 yards beyond the church turn left over a stile and follow a field edge. After about 200 yards, go forward through a gap and bear left along a left field edge. Walk round two sides of this field, descending into a dip. As you climb again, look out for a stile on the left into woods. In 50 yards turn left, downhill, and at the bottom keep straight on, ignoring a right fork, and climb. At a T-junction turn right and descend, following the path out of the wood and along the left hand edge of a large field. At the bottom corner of this field continue ahead into woodland again and follow the main track which curves right, then left and uphill through the wood. Towards the top cross over an oblique crossing track and emerge from the wood to pass two cottages on your left.

Soon after passing the second cottage (Keepers Cottage) keep straight on at a T-junction on a tree-lined path which soon enters woodland. Ignore all crossing tracks and descend to cross a road in the valley.

Go straight across the road and ahead up the left hand edge of a field. After passing under power lines, follow a clear track half left into woods

21

and uphill. Once again, ignore all side tracks and follow the main path for ⅔ mile into Stoughton village. The church is on the left just before reaching the road in the village and is well worth visiting. Some of the original Saxon work remains including an impressive chancel arch.

At the road turn left, passing the Hare and Hounds public house on the left and in about 600 yards (about 200 yards beyond the last house on the left), turn left on an enclosed track which climbs towards a belt of woodland. Just short of the woods, turn right over a stile and follow along the edge of the wooded area with views across the valley to Bow Hill. At the corner of the field go straight ahead into the sparse remains of Inholmes Wood, devastated in the 1987 gale. Your path now keeps approximately along the contour in the same general direction (north-northeast) for ¾ mile. Keep at about the same height along the valley, finally joining your outgoing route and turning right to descend to the road. Here turn right and return to the car park.

(To link with Walk 4 go through a field gate at the northern corner of the car park and follow a roughly metalled track for 450 yards round the shoulder of Lambdown Hill.)

KINGLEY VALE

WALK 6

★

4 or 5½ miles (6.5 or 9 km)

OS Landranger sheet 197

This is a fairly short walk through what has been described as 'the finest yew forest in Europe', and climbing to the top of Bow Hill with fine views into Hampshire and across the Chichester creeks to the sea and the Isle of Wight. The walk can be extended by linking it with Walk 4 as indicated in the route description.

Kingley Vale is now protected by the Nature Conservancy Council. It is an area of great beauty and interest, and not only to naturalists. A section of the walk follows part of a Nature Trail passing the oldest yew trees, now 500 years old, and then climbing up through the younger part of the forest where the trees are up to 100 years old, offspring of the ancient yews in the valley.

Bow Hill is a very ancient spot. On the top four Bronze Age barrows, known as the Devil's Humps, stand beside an ancient trackway — two bell barrows to the south-west, which are visible for miles around, and two bowl barrows to the north-east. The whole area is rich in earthworks, including an Iron Age farmstead and possibly some Neolithic flint mines.

Park at the Kingley Vale car park which is situated on the unclassified road to the north of East Ashling and west of West Stoke. To reach it turn right (north) off the B2178 Chichester to Petersfield road where it makes a sharp right-angled turn in the village of East Ashling 3 miles north-west of Chichester (OS map ref. 820079). The car park is on the right in ¾ mile, just beyond a road junction at OS map ref. 824087.

From the car park go over a stile by a metal gate and follow a roughly metalled track for ¾ mile to the foot of Kingley Vale. Keep straight on, passing to the left of the Field Centre (well worth a visit if open) and follow part of the signposted and numbered Nature Trail (for which a very well produced guide is available from a dispenser) for another ¾ mile to the top of Bow Hill with its two prominent bell barrows. Go right up to these two mounds on the summit before doubling back to the right along the top of the hill, passing immediately to the right of two more barrows and a flint viewpoint table. There are fine views northwards to the Downs escarpment from Linch Down to Butser Hill and southwards to Chichester and the Isle of Wight.

Follow a clear track eastwards and, soon after passing a triangulation point half hidden in the scrub on your left, turn sharp right downhill on a crossing track by a Nature Reserve notice (this is the link point for Walk 4). Drop down on a sunken track from which there are views ahead to Stoke Clump and Chichester cathedral beyond. At the bottom of the hill, after passing another Nature Reserve notice, go straight ahead on a fenced track between fields. In just over ¼ mile turn right at a crossing track and follow it back to cross your outgoing route at the foot of Kingley Vale. (To return directly to the car park on the 4 mile walk, turn left here.)

To continue the 5½ mile walk, keep straight ahead past another Nature Reserve notice and follow a path between fences over the shoulder of Stoke Down and downhill past an old quarry for nearly a mile to reach the road at Woodend.

At the road turn right, and in 100 yards turn left. Ignore the first track into woodland on the left but after another 180 yards, where a track crosses the road, turn left through a gate and follow a straight woodland path. Ignore all side tracks for ½ mile and then, about 50 yards beyond a wide crossing track (signposted at the time of writing), fork left on an oblique crossing track, follow this out to a road and turn left. In 150 yards at a T-junction, turn left and return to the car park.

SINGLETON AND EAST DEAN

WALK 7

★

6½ miles (10.5 km)

OS Landranger sheet 197

Goodwood is often claimed to be the most picturesque racecourse in the British Isles. Although it would certainly be wise to avoid attempting this walk on a race day, at other times the course, set 500 feet up into the Downs, is as good a place as any to begin a downland walk.

This one starts by climbing to the Trundle, an impressive Iron Age hill-fort encircling the summit of St. Roche's Hill, so called because it was the site of a medieval chapel. From the top, there are magnificent views across the coastal plain towards the sea with the Isle of Wight on the horizon. In the foreground can be seen the spire of Chichester cathedral and the shining pattern of the creeks of Chichester harbour stretched out towards Hayling Island.

The walk continues by descending to the neat and prosperous looking village of Singleton. From here a short detour from the described route will take you to the Weald and Downland open air museum. This is a unique collection of old buildings, mostly rescued from almost certain destruction on their original sites in various parts of southern England, and painstakingly re-erected on the spacious museum site in West Dean park. One building, Bayleaf, is a superb 15th century hall from the Weald, and other exhibits include a 14th century farmhouse and a 19th century toll cottage. A charcoal burners' camp has been reconstructed as part of a woodland nature trail.

After climbing over Levin Down and Court Hill, the walk descends to the small village of East Dean, set, like Singleton, in a downland valley. The final climb through East Dean park brings you back to Goodwood.

Park in the large car parking area at Goodwood country park which is situated immediately to the south of Goodwood racecourse. To get there, turn north off the A27 road at the roundabout at the eastern end of the Chichester bypass. Turn right just before reaching the racecourse buildings. The car park is on the right after passing the grandstand (OS map ref. 885110).

From the car park follow the road westwards past the grandstand. At a T-junction (signposted Singleton and Midhurst) turn right. After 300 yards, with the grandstands now on your right, turn left along a metalled drive, once a loop of the old road. After 50 yards, fork left on a chalky path, soon with metal railings on your right. Where the bridleway curves away to the left round the flank of the hill, take a footpath which keeps close to the railings and climbs to the Trundle on the top. After encircling the ramparts, preferably in a clockwise direction to obtain all the available views, drop down northwards with metal railings on your right and go straight across a triangular parking area to follow a narrow road into the valley.

In 500 yards, go over a stile on the left and cross a large field, diverging gradually from the road and aiming for a gap in the near hills, through which, on a clear day, you can catch a glimpse of the distant Weald. Soon the village of Singleton comes into view, tucked down in the valley, and provides a more immediate objective. Pick up a fence on your right and follow it down to Singleton church, which is reached through a frequently very muddy farmyard. Go round the church in a clockwise direction within the churchyard wall. From the far left corner of the churchyard, turn left through a gate and out to the road by the Fox and Hounds public house in Singleton village. (To visit the Weald and Downland open-air museum turn left here.)

To continue the walk, turn right along the road. At a junction keep straight on, signposted Charlton and East Dean, and in 150 yards, immediately after crossing the Lavant stream, turn left between school and graveyard and climb up on to Levin Down. Where the hedge on

26

the left ends, veer slightly right to a stile which can be seen in the hedge on the skyline. A few yards beyond this hedge, go right on a bridleway which curves rather indistinctly round the left flank of Levin Down (ignore a signposted crossing track). Beyond a field gate there is little to guide you, but you should follow the side of the hill round, staying approximately at the same contour level, eventually walking parallel to and about 200 yards away from a belt of woodland to the left. Now aim downhill for a substantial carved oak waypost which has, unfortunately lost all its direction arms. At the post, bear right, to follow a clear chalk track downhill with Levin Down now rising steeply up on the right. At the bottom curve left with the path and in 50 yards, at a T-junction, turn left.

Now follow this clear flint track, North Lane, which curves round the flank of North Down to the right and continues up the floor of a valley for more than ½ mile. At a Forestry Commission notice 'Charlton Forest' and five yards short of a gate, turn right on a narrow path, and along the left hand edge of a short section of open downland before climbing on a grassy track through a plantation of conifers. Go straight over two wide grassy rides before entering deciduous woodland and going straight over a crossing track. At the top edge of the woodland the footpath keeps straight on over the open downland, but if it is ploughed and planted it may be easiest to follow the often well trodden path round the left hand side of the field along the edge of the woodland. After crossing a stile, where the edge of the woodland drops away more steeply to the left, keep straight on over the open downland, soon veering gradually left towards a line of trees down the hill on your left. Converge on this line of trees at a stile and gate and go ahead with the line of trees to the left, now on a clear track which soon descends in a hollow way between banks. Follow this round to the left, down to a road and turn right.

In a little over 100 yards, tun right at a T-junction and descend into East Dean village. After passing the Hurdlemakers public house, ignore a turning to the left, and after passing a pond on the right, fork left (signposted to Goodwood and Chichester). Climb out of the village and in about 250 yards, immediately after passing under power lines, fork right on a chalky track. Follow a fence line which keeps parallel to the power lines. In 150 yards go over a stile and turn left to climb the shoulder of Park Hill to enter a wooded area over a stile by a gate. Keep to the left hand side of an open space on the top of the hill, then cross a stile beside a gate to follow a clearer track through more woodland and out to a road. Turn right at the road and return along it for ¾ mile to the car park. There is room to walk on the wide grass verge to the left of the road.

Barlavington Hanger

Walk 10

Barlavington Down

Duncton Hanger

A285

Car Park

Dog Kennel Cottages

START

Duncton Down

Beechwood Lane

Fryans Hanger

A285

Littleton Farm

Beechwood House

Beech Cottage

Seaford College

Littleton Down

Woolavington Down

SOUTH DOWNS WAY

Old Walk 8

Graffham Down

Old Walk 8

N ←

GRAFFHAM DOWN, BARLAVINGTON HILL AND DUNCTON HANGER

WALK 8

★

6¼ miles (10km)

OS Landranger Sheet 197

This fairly energetic walk is new to this edition and explores a thickly wooded section of the Downs which juts out into the Weald to the south of Petworth. From a starting point half way up the hill, the route descends to hug the foot of the wooded scarp slope before climbing steeply on to Graffham Down. This summit area too, was once well wooded but was cleared and cultivated a few years ago in spite of protests from conservationists. The whole sorry saga is described in detail in Marion Shoard's book *The Theft of the Countryside*.

After a mile on the South Downs Way, the walk uses an ancient green lane, part of an old road over the Downs to Sutton, before crossing the shoulder of Barlavington Down and dropping down into woodland once more. The last half mile traverses the side of Duncton Hanger where many fine beeches were miraculously preserved from the ravages of the 1987 gale.

This walk can be linked with Walk 10 to provide a combined figure-of-eight circuit totalling just over 15 miles. Also, for about ¼ mile along the foot of Graffham Down, the walk duplicates a section of the ramble, numbered 8 in earlier editions of this book, and starting from Lavington Common to the north. These two circuits, if combined, provide a nicely contrasted walk of just over 11 miles in all.

Park at the car park, picnic site and viewpoint which can be found to the right of the A285, Petworth to Chichester road, half way up the Downs escarpment at Duncton Down (OS map ref. 954161).

Start the walk along the path from the upper end of the car park. It climbs a few steps and then runs parallel to the road, a few yards to the left. At a T-Junction, turn left, still climbing. After about 30 yards, fork right, now gradually diverging from the road and soon losing height.

A clear path descends through coppiced woodland. At the bottom of the hill, walk out past a cottage, using a gravelled drive which passes an ornamental lake, to join a lane. Turn left and after ¼ mile, just past Beech Cottage on the right, where the lane veers right through a gate into the grounds of Seaford College, you should go ahead, now on a roughly metalled track which climbs gently, soon with a high flint wall to the right.

At a Y-junction with a chalky track, fork right on the lower path, still with a wall to your right. Go straight over a crossing track and ahead, with the buildings of Seaford College visible away to the right of the path. A track continues along the foot of the Downs escarpment, thickly wooded, mainly beech and yew.

After another ¼ mile, at a junction of four paths, go almost directly ahead, ignoring a narrow path which forks right, downhill. Where another bridleway goes left, steeply up on to the Downs, go ahead once more. You are now on part of the walk numbered 8 in earlier editions of this book.

After looping round a shallow combe, you will come to a meeting of five ways. The old walk 8 forks right down into Graffham, but this walk continues ahead on a narrow path, soon beneath minor power lines. Where the power lines veer right, you should turn left on a crossing path which climbs steeply up through the trees.

Go straight over a chalky track and climb the even steeper path opposite. The gradient eases as the path veers left and climbs obliquely up the side of the wooded scarp slope, indistinct in places. At the top, where the walk comes out into the open for the first time, bear left on a clear track for a few yards only before going right through a bridle gate and half left across the open summit of Graffham Down where the path is liable to be ploughed out and may be vague or absent.

On the other side of the field, bear left on a clear track, part of the South Downs Way, which you should now follow for over a mile. After ½ mile or so you will come to Tegleaze Post where the view back across Bexley Hill to the wooded heights of Blackdown, is superb. You are within a few hundred yards of the highest point on the Downs at Crown Tegleaze.

The South Downs Way continues through a copse and then descends, unfenced, across Littleton Down with more wide views ahead to Bignor Hill. Towards the bottom of the hill where the South Downs Way enters an enclosed track as it approaches the A285 road, you should turn left on a wide track along the side of the valley, with a line of trees to your right.

After 600 yards, turn right on a track which leads out to the A285 at Dogkennel Cottages. Cross the main road and turn left, past a telephone box, and ahead on a redundant loop of the old A285. Where this narrows and peters out after 100 yards or so, turn right on an unsignposted chalk and flint track which is the old road which crossed the Downs to Sutton. It is not marked as a right of way on OS maps but is still a public highway.

After ½ mile, where this green lane reaches its highest point, you should turn left on a clear crossing track. This is the link point with Walk 10. Ignore two paths to the right, the second of which is used on Walk 10 and soon climb steeply up and over the shoulder of Barlavington Hill, shortly with newly planted trees to the right.

A well placed seat provides an excuse to get your breath and look back along the line of the Downs escarpment to the east. As well as the wireless masts on Bignor Hill, you should be able to identify the Amberley chalk pits to the east of the Arun gap, the stunted remains of Chanctonbury Ring (Walk 17) and, in the far distance, the profile of Wolstonbury Hill (Walk 21), 20 miles away.

The walk continues along the upper edge of Barlavington Hanger before dropping down into Duncton Woods. Once within the woods, look out for a narrow signposted bridleway to the left which takes a level course to a T-junction where you should turn right, downhill.

After another 150 yards, at a meeting of five paths, turn sharply back to the left (in roundabout terms, the 'first exit'). An undulating track traverses the side of Duncton Hanger for ½ mile. Where the bridleway is signposted on a right, downhill, fork, go ahead, still on a clear track, unofficial but well used. This track takes you back to the A285 opposite the car park.

WALK 9

To Petworth

Ch

UP WALTHAM

N

To East Dean

F.C. Notice

Narrow Cleared Strip

DROKE

A 285

Small F.C. Car Park

Selhurst Park

F.C. Notice

Cleared Area

To Walk 1

Selhurst Park Farm

Footpath on agger

A 285

Eartham Wood

Stane Street

Gumber Farm

A 285

To Chichester

Meeting of 6 Bridleways

Start

Park Here

STANE STREET

WALK 9

★

9 miles (13 km)

OS Landranger sheet 197

This is one of the longer and more strenuous walks through undulating and mainly wooded downland. It includes a 2½ mile stretch of Roman road as well as some pleasant sheltered forest rides through young Forestry Commission beechwoods and an open section across Selhurst Park with views to the coastal plain. A waymarked Forestry Commission forest trail starts from the car park at the beginning of the walk. Walks 9 and 10 may be linked as indicated in the route description to give an energetic 18-mile circuit.

Park at the Forestry Commission car park at Eartham Wood which is reached by forking left off the A285 Petworth to Chichester road about 4 miles south of Duncton and 7 miles north-east of Chichester. The large parking area is on the left in less than ½ mile from the turn-off (OS map ref. 939106).

From the car park take a fenced path which starts between wooden posts at the end of the first 'bay' on the right inside the entrance. In about 150 yards turn right on a Forestry road and after another 60 yards, by a National Trust notice, double back to the left on a roughly metalled track which follows the line of Stane Street. Continue through Eartham Wood for about a mile, ignoring all side and crossing tracks. At a meeting of six bridleways where there is a substantial carved oak way post, keep straight on out of the forest area to follow one of the best preserved sections of the Roman road.

Stane Street linked London and Chichester and is clearly visible as it crosses the Downs between Bignor Hill and the A285 road below Halnaker Hill, aligned with the spire of Chichester cathedral. Now covered with grass, the *agger* was built with a foundation of rammed flint and chalk capped with flint and gravel. Traces of the drainage ditches on either side can be seen in a few places.

After about ¾ mile and fairly soon after passing Gumber Farm away to the right, footpath and bridleway divide and run parallel. It is pleasanter to keep left on the footpath which follows the line of the Roman *agger* and is narrow in places. Finally, immediately after crossing a stile, go sharp left and follow a clear track westwards for a mile. (To link with Walk 10 keep straight on along Stane Street to the top of Bignor Hill.)

Keep going westwards on the track which has been churned up by timber hauling, until, about 60 yards short of a Forestry Commission notice 'Eartham Wood', you should turn right. In a few yards only fork left and very shortly fork right, to pass through a planted area, now heading north. Soon the path follows along the right hand edge of a field with forestry plantation to the right, and then goes ahead across open downland descending into the valley at Up Waltham. On reaching a farm, turn left to follow a signposted footpath round to the left of the main buildings and out to the A285 road.

Up Waltham is a tiny flint and tile hamlet with a lovely little downland church, simple and basically unaltered since the 13th century. Cardinal Manning, the Roman Catholic Archbishop of Westminster in late Victorian times, was rector here before 'changing sides'.

To visit the church, which was until fairly recently lit by candles in chandeliers, turn right along the road for a few yards. Access is along a track which starts on the left of the road by a square flint building. But to continue the walk turn left along the A285 for about 200 yards, and then, just beyond a cottage on the left, go right over a stile and climb, on to Waltham Down. Keep to the right of a field at first, then join a track between two fields. After a stile beside a gate, follow the meandering right hand edge of a large field for about 3/4 mile, with woodland dropping away to the right.

At the top corner of this field go ahead over a stile into woodland. In another few yards turn left on a wider track which soon opens out to become a broad fire break. In a little over 1/4 mile, at a clearing where a number of ways meet, turn left on a clear track. In another 1/4 mile, just before the main track curves left, fork right, soon joining a broader track coming in from the left. Follow this forest track downhill, continuing straight on when the main track forks right. Soon, go ahead through a bridle gate and bear slightly right across a cleared strip to re-enter woodland and descend to the road at Droke.

Turn left along the road for about 100 yards before going right, immediately short of a car parking area. Now ignore all side tracks and climb for nearly half a mile through an afforested area to the Selhurst Park road. Go straight across the road and over a stile, then strike out half left across Selhurst Park, passing about 100 yards to the right of an isolated group of trees.

There are fine views over the coastal plain and across to the prominent hilltop landmark of Halnaker Mill, a solid brick tower structure, built in 1750, restored in 1934, and still with sweeps and fantail.

On reaching a belt of scrub, go left along the edge. Where the scrub ends, veer half right, aiming for a stile in the far field corner. Beyond the stile, head across a field, passing close to an isolated tree to join Selhurst Park farm access track. Turn left along this and follow it out to the A285 road.

Go straight across the road, continue on a clear track through to another road and turn right to return to the car park.

BIGNOR HILL AND BARLAVINGTON

WALK 10

★

9 miles (13 km)

OS Landranger sheet 197

This is a fairly long but very fine walk which starts off through the Forestry Commission area of Houghton Forest but then climbs to the top of Bignor Hill before following a splendid section along the edge of the Downs escarpment inexplicably eschewed by the planners of the official South Downs Way in favour of a much inferior route further to the south. The return journey traverses the foothills of the Downs and passes through the villages of Sutton and Bignor (with an opportunity to visit the Roman villa) before climbing back over Westburton Hill. This walk may be linked with Walk 9 to give a combined circuit of 18 miles, or with Walk 8 to provide 15 miles in all.

Park in the large car park at Whiteways Lodge at the junction of the A29 and A284 roads about 3 miles north of Arundel (OS map ref. 001109).

Leave the car park along a track about 50 yards to the right of the refreshment kiosk. Go straight ahead past a Forestry Commission notice 'Houghton Forest' and on through a gap beside a gate. In about 500 yards fork left and then ignore all turnings to right and left for just over a mile. Leave the forest and go ahead with an open field on your right and a plantation to the left. Towards the end of this field the path crosses the site of Barkhale, a Neolithic causewayed camp — one of only four in the South Downs area, the other three being at the Trundle, Goodwood (Walk 7), Coombe Hill, Jevington (Walk 30) and Whitehawk, Brighton. Barkhale has been largely obliterated by ploughing.

Where the field on the right ends, turn right on a crossing track and ascend to the National Trust open space at Bignor Post. You are now at over 700 feet above sea level and there are fine views northwards over the Weald and eastwards along the Downs to Chanctonbury Ring and Wolstonbury Hill beyond. The Roman road Stane Street crosses the line of the walk a little to the west of this point and the signpost on the summit reminds us that it was the direct route from Londinium to Regnum (Chichester).

From Bignor Post follow the South Downs Way westwards on a chalky track aiming towards two radio masts and in about 200 yards keep right, crossing the line of Stane Street. (To link with Walk 9 turn left and follow the line of Stane Street.)

Pass to the right of the radio masts, ignoring two tracks to the left, and begin gradually to drop downhill. In just under ½ mile and a few yards before the main track curves away to the left (not a right of way), turn right through an area of scrub, and in about 30 yards, where the track divides into three, keep to the leftmost fork. Your path now follows a line of trees and then curves to the right along the top edge of woodland on the right and the flank of Farm Hill on the left. Ignore a right fork which follows the edge of the woodland downhill and instead keep straight ahead on a track which crosses open downland and drops down over a large field. Go over a crossing track, the link point with Walk 8, ignore the first track on the right into woods in 30 yards, but 10 yards further on fork right on a clear grassy bridleway. This fine terraced path drops down into the valley at Barlavington. Towards the bottom the official bridle route keeps outside the woodland to the right, but pedestrians may go over a stile and are normally permitted to use the fine hollow way which drops down within the woodland.

At the bottom go straight across a road and follow the access road to Barlavington church, a simple 13th century structure beside a farmyard with a fine view of the thickly wooded Downs.

Take a footpath which keeps round to the south of the church within the churchyard. After leaving the churchyard, skirt to the right of some farm buildings on a clear track and then turn right, on a wide grassy path, enclosed at first. Near the bottom of the hill go over a stile in the hedge on your right and descend across a meadow skirting to the right of a partially dried up pond, to cross a stream. In 10 yards keep right and climb up through a narrow belt of woodland and over a stile into a field.

Now ascend along the left hand edge of this field, ignoring a path off to the left about two-thirds of the way up, and where the ground levels out strike out half left on a path which is usually trodden out through the crop. (To visit Sutton's 12th to 14th century church with its fine shingled cap, turn left instead of going diagonally across the field — to rejoin the walk turn right on the road through the village to the White Horse public house.) At the far side of the field go over a stile and cross a lawn to enter a narrow path which leads to the road at the White Horse.

At the road turn right and in a few yards at a T-junction go almost straight ahead on a path to the right of a thatched cottage and out into a field. Go straight out across this field, downhill, over a stile and on to a wooden gate and a bridge over a stream. Now keep left on a winding track through woodland. Recross the stream by a plank bridge and climb to a road. Turn right along the road and follow it round to the left through the village of Bignor. Alternatively, to see the best of the village turn left and follow the 'square' of roads round as shown on the sketch map. Bignor is a village with two famous buildings — The Old Shop, a much photographed 15th century cottage at the eastern end of the village, and one of the largest Roman Villas in England. This was uncovered by the plough in 1811, first excavated in 1827, and contains some magnificent tessellated pavement in beautifully clear colours. Its location is also indicated on the sketch map.

Leave the village along the road to the Downs. If you have not made a detour to visit the village or the villa, it is simply a matter, having climbed to the road from the ford, of turning right, following the road round to the left and in 200 yards turning right at a staggered crossroads. Follow the road to the Downs past a farm and upwards for about $1/4$ mile. Where the road turns fairly sharply to the right, go straight ahead on a bridleway, in 50 yards keeping right to follow the main track upwards for something over $1/2$ mile (ignore a right fork), finally descending to join the South Downs Way. Here, go straight ahead passing to the right of three adjacent barns and climb over the flank of Westburton Hill with fine views opening out to Highdown Hill (Walk 15) and the sea beyond.

In about a mile the path converges on woodland to the right. Where this woodland ends, turn right and follow a clear track with a large field on your left and a belt of woodland on your right. In $2/3$ mile cut through the corner of woodland to pick up and rejoin the outgoing route at the entrance to Houghton Forest. Turn left and return to the car park.

SLINDON WOODS

WALK 11

★

5½ miles (9km)

OS Landranger sheet 197

When this walk was first conceived in 1980, the magnificent beeches of Slindon Park provided the main feature of this pleasant downland walk which passes through the National Trust Slindon estate of 3503 acres. During one night in October 1987, the entire wood was virtually destroyed by gale force winds. The debris has now been cleared away and, by 1992, regeneration and replanting were well under way. The estate stretches to the northern foot of the Downs beyond Bignor Hill and Glatting Beacon. Slindon is a well-kept village, most of which also belongs to the National Trust. It contains a much restored church with a splendid carved wooden effigy of a 16th century knight in armour, the only one like it in Sussex.

Park in the National Trust car park at Slindon Woods. Turn left (north) from the Fontwell bypass on the A27 Worthing to Chichester road on to the A29. In a few yards, fork left on an unclassified road and in another ⅓ mile, park at a woodland National Trust car park on the left at OS map ref. 961077.

To orientate yourself for the start of the walk, return to the car park entrance and turn round to face into the car parking area. Now go left (south-west) on a broad track which starts through a gate. Follow this wide path for ⅓ mile until, at a meeting of four paths, you should turn right, still on the main track. In 60 yards, go straight over a crossing track and soon join and bear right on another broad track. After ½ mile, double back sharply to the left downhill, then in 150 yards turn right and in another 75 yards right again to follow a clear path along a valley, ignoring a right fork, to join a road over a stile.

At the road turn left and in about 100 yards turn right on an enclosed bridleway which climbs for more than a mile to the top of Nore Hill. The building on the hill away to the right as you climb is Nore Folly, built as a summer house and apparently intended for shooting lunches. It is now a ruin. Ignore all side turnings and keep to the main track which can be very muddy. Towards the top a view to the north begins to open out on the left of the path. Keep going until you get to a clear rutted track on which you should turn sharply back to the left, dropping down into the valley. At the first crossing track turn right and in about 200 yards right again. In ⅓ mile join and bear right on a wider farm access track and follow it out to a farm road by a National Trust notice 'North Wood'.

Here turn right. After about 300 yards along the road fork left along a dirt track through a narrow belt of woodland and ahead, uphill, along a wide fenced track. Keep straight on through a strip of woodland. At the far side of the wooded strip turn right and follow a wide track within the left hand edge of the wooded area.

(To link with Walk 12 soon bear left with the fence line on your left and in 100 yards turn left, signposted 'Bridle road to Bignor', on a clear path across a large field — see map.)

To continue with this walk, however, keep right following the main track and passing a barn on the right after 200 yards. Now follow this track for nearly ½ mile out to a road and turn left, soon passing Slindon House on your right.

In the centre of the village fork right soon passing Slindon church on the right. Immediately after passing a pond on the right, turn sharp right along the edge of the pond and enter Slindon Woods by a National Trust notice. Just inside the woods, where the path forks, keep left and follow a clear track, forking left again to return to the car park.

REWELL WOOD AND SLINDON

WALK 12

★

5½ miles (9 km)

OS Landranger sheet 197

A walk through thickly wooded downland and visiting the attractive village of Slindon (see Walk 11). There is a fine open stretch over Little Down.

Madehurst is a tiny hamlet beautifully set in wooded country at the end of a cul-de-sac. The name means 'Speech Wood', probably because the Moot, an early form of local government was held in the parish at a spot called Nonemanneslond ('No man's land'), recorded in 1361.

The church looks interesting but is largely a Victorian rebuilding, with a Norman west door. It contains a number of memorials to the family who lived in the great house (demolished in 1959) of nearby Dale Park.

Fairmile Bottom is a wide and beautiful valley, somewhat marred by the busy A29 road running through it. West Sussex County Council owns and manages a 120 acre public open space and picnic area on the south-east side of the valley, partly open grassland and partly beech and yew woodland. A mile-long Nature Trail starts from the same point as this walk (though it follows a different route) and is laid out with 17 numbered stopping places. If you would like to add it to the beginning or end of the walk, an informative leaflet guide is available from a dispenser at the beginning of the trail.

Walks 11 and 12 can be combined to form a figure-of-eight circuit of 11 miles (or 12 with the Nature Trail). Details of the short link between the walks is given in the route description.

Park behind the Fairmile Bottom Café (OS map ref. 991097) on the south-east side of the A29 about 3 miles north-east of Fontwell.

The Nature Trail follows a circular route up the valley, but to follow the described walk, start from the café by walking *down* the valley in a south-westerly direction. The path starts from the end of the car park and runs parallel to the A29, within woodland at first, then across an open grassy slope, still parallel to but well above the road. After about ½ mile look out for a crossing track which starts from the road by a white notice board. Turn left on this track which climbs steeply out of the valley through some yews. Near the top of the hill go over a crossing track and in about 150 yards, at a point where six ways meet, take the first path to the right and keep to the main track through Rewell Wood, ignoring all side tracks for ¾ mile. The wood is full of earthworks which have been the subject of much archaeological speculation. It may have been the site of a sort of Celtic city.

At a meeting of five ways turn right (just north of west) downhill, ignoring both an immediate right fork and a left turn after 75 yards. In the valley where a number of paths join, keep straight on along the main track, but where the main path starts to climb gently, opposite a gate leading to a wooden hut, take a narrower path which forks to the left. In 50 yards go over a stile into a field. Go straight ahead across this field and over two more stiles to reach the main A29 road.

Go straight across the road and up some steps to follow a clear path to the Newburgh Arms public house in Slindon. At the road keep right past the post office and in 100 yards turn right. In another 250 yards where the road goes right keep straight ahead on a rutted track which climbs at first and then drops down through a belt of woodland. Towards the bottom of the woodland fork right and cross an open piece of ground to a gate leading into a large field. (To link with Walk 11 do not go through this gate but bear left with a fence on your right for about 100 yards before doubling back to the left on a wide track.)

To continue with Walk 12 go through the gate and follow a clear fenced track, signposted 'Bridle Road to Bignor', across the middle of the large open area of Little Down. In about ⅔ mile, immediately beyond a line of trees, turn right over a stile and follow the field edge down into a dip, over two more stiles and up again beside a wood. At the top of a rise, go left through a gate and strike out half left across

41

the next field, converging on a fence line on your left and following it to a gate in the top left hand corner of the field.

Immediately beyond this gate turn sharp left on a hard track which curves to the right and soon joins a metalled road. Follow this to a T-junction where turn right. This road takes you down into a valley and then uphill bearing right at a junction to reach the tiny hamlet of Madehurst. Just beyond a telephone box where the road turns right keep straight on along a rough track which leads into a field over a stile. Keep along the right hand edge of this field and the next, dropping down into Fairmile Bottom and climbing again to the A29 and the start of the walk.

PERRY HILL AND BURPHAM

WALK 13

★

6½ miles (9.5 km)

OS Landranger sheet 197

This is a fine open downland walk, starting at a height of over 600 feet and dropping down to less than 100 feet in the Arun valley. There are superb views across the river to Arundel Park and beyond where the Downs become more wooded for the last 18 miles or so to the Hampshire border.

Burpham is an unspoilt village at the end of a lane which goes nowhere else. The name, from the Old English *Burh Ham*, means a 'settlement by a stronghold', and earthworks to the south of the church are the remains of the Saxon fort built by King Alfred to defend the river valley against the Danes. The fort may have been surrounded by tidal waters at that date. The church is partly Norman in origin, perhaps earlier. Part of a Roman pavement was uncovered by grave-digging in the late 19th century.

Park at Parham Post (OS map ref. 070125) which can be reached along a 'No Through Road' which leaves the B2139 road about 1½ miles south-west of Storrington and climbs to the top of the Downs, where there is a large parking area.

From the car park cross over the South Downs Way and follow a broad track which descends gently in a south-westerly direction, soon with an area of scrub on the right, and views ahead to the coastal plain. Where the scrubby area ends keep straight on with a fence on your left, still on a clear track. Immediately short of a copse ahead turn right and cross a short section of open field to a crossing track where turn left.

In 300 yards ignore two tracks to the right and continue ahead over the low summit of Wepham Down. In another 400 yards, just short of the point where the track ahead acquires a metalled surface, turn sharply back to the right on a track which curves left and climbs to the top of Perry Hill, where there are extensive views southwards over the coastal plain, westwards over the Arun Valley to Arundel Park and Castle and north-westwards to Bexley Hill and Blackdown on the Surrey border. A path dropping down the hill to the right (not used on the present walk) runs on the line of the so-called 'Lepers Path' which linked a leper settlement on the site of Angmering Lea Farm to the east with the chapel of St. James which stood near Offham in the Arun valley until the 15th century.

When the path forks near the top of the hill, keep right and follow

43

the shoulder of Perry Hill with the village of Burpham spread out below in the valley to the right. At a T-junction keep right and drop down to the road in the tiny hamlet of Wepham. Turn right along the road for 80 yards and then take a concrete track to the left. In 60 yards, keep to the right of a thatched barn and in a few more yards go right over a stile and round to the right of a second thatched barn. Now drop down across a field, go over a stile, and bear right down a flight of steps to a stream crossing and on to a road where you turn right and climb, ignoring a right turn, to reach the George and Dragon public house in the village of Burpham.

Go into the churchyard opposite the pub and keep round to the right of the church. Do not go through a gap in the wall on the right but climb three steps and go over a low section of wall ahead to follow a narrow path between fence and hedge. Where the enclosed section of the path ends, continue ahead along the field edge to a road and turn left. In 250 yards, go ahead along the access track to the farm buildings at Peppering High Barn. Keep round to the left of the farm buildings and then fork right up a concrete track which continues to curve past the buildings and a silage pit and then becomes a dirt track, between fences at first and then with a fence to the right.

44

Now keep straight ahead for 3 miles, climbing gently and ignoring all paths to the right and left, finally reaching the South Downs Way at the top of the scarp slope just to the left of a clump of trees which can be seen on the skyline as you ascend. Turn right on the South Downs Way from which there are splendid views over the Weald. Tucked under the Downs can be seen the magnificent Elizabethan mansion of Parham, built in 1580 and carefully restored early in the present century. It is set in a 500 acre deer park and is open to the public on certain days during the summer months.

Follow the South Downs Way for a little over ½ mile back to the car park.

HAMMERPOT AND PATCHING HILL

WALK 14

★

6½ miles (10.5 km)

OS Landranger sheet 197

Although longer than some in this book this is not a strenuous walk and passes through a mostly wooded stretch of the southern slope of the Downs where they begin to climb gently up from the coastal plain. It reaches a height of 468 feet on Barpham Hill, with views across miles of downland and also over the Arun valley to Arundel Park and Castle, only 3 miles away. The path through Patching Woods can be extremely muddy.

Patching is an attractive village of flint and thatch. The church is plain and bare, with a good timber roof and a handsome shingled spire.

This walk can be combined with Walk 15 to give a round trip of about 13½ miles. The linking route is included with the walk description and indicated on the sketch map.

Park on the redundant loop of the old A27 road at Hammerpot. This is now a cul-de-sac to the left (north) of the A27 Arundel-Worthing road, three miles east of Arundel, and forms the access road to the Woodmans Arms public house (OS map ref. 067057). There is a grass verge which provides adequate but not ample parking space.

Start the walk by going north on a enclosed bridleway which leaves the cul-de-sac road immediately to the west of the Woodmans Arms car park. Follow this path for 100 yards only before turning right over a stile and a plank bridge into a field. Now go straight ahead with a ditch on your left for 500 yards to join a roughly metalled track.

Turn left along this track for less than 100 yards before going right on a narrow path along the edge of woodland. Beyond the wood, strike out diagonally across a field, aiming for some brick buildings which may just be seen through a line of trees. Go through a gap in this line of trees and ahead between fences to join a farm track.

Turn left, and after 250 yards, where woodland begins on the left of the path, turn right on a flinty track with a hedge on your right at first, then across an open field, aiming for the right hand end of a strip of woodland. The path then winds through the end of this narrow belt of woodland and crosses a field, aiming towards farm buildings a little to the right of Patching church. Immediately short of the farm buildings turn sharply back to the left and follow a wide flint track.

(To link with Walk 15, keep ahead through the farm buildings and then turn right down the village street. In 100 yards turn left opposite a letter-box and follow a narrow road for ¼ mile. At a T-junction turn right and in 200 yards, about 50 yards beyond a left turn to Clapham village, turn left on a narrow metalled driveway lined on the right with a row of lime trees. You are now on Walk 15.)

To continue with Walk 14 follow the flint track for ¼ mile before turning right at a T-junction, still on a clear track between fences. In 200 yards go through a field gate on to the flat top of Patching Hill. From this point there are extensive views, south to Highdown Hill and Clapham village with glimpses of Worthing and the sea beyond, and north-east where Chanctonbury Ring can be seen on the crest of the Downs.

Immediately beyond the field gate turn left along the top of Patching Hill with a hedge on the left. After about 600 yards, pass through a scattered clump of trees, bearing slightly right, away from the hedge, and go over a stile into woods. The path into the woodland is laid with hardcore at first but soon becomes a soft and often muddy track. Go straight over a crossing track and follow a bridleway, much poached by horses. Go over another and broader crossing track. For a while the path is fenced on the right; there is a turning to the left which should be ignored. At an oblique crossing track fork right and shortly, at a Y-junction, turn right again. In 50 yards go straight across a clearing, ignoring a track through a gate to the right, and after passing through another strip of woodland, go ahead with a fence and woodland to the right and open downland to the left.

After passing through another field gate, bear immediately left on a well trodden track which follows the same contour along the hillside with views across the valley to the Neolithic flint mines on the top of Harrow Hill and a further glimpse of Chanctonbury Ring in the distance.

Follow this fine terraced track for about ¾ mile. Immediately after passing through a field gate and under telephone wires, bear left in a slightly sunken way, before turning right to cross a farm track and climb to a bridle gate beside a double field gate. A few yards beyond the gate, fork left from the main track with a line of hawthorn trees and a fence to your left and a triangulation point a little way away to the right on the top of the hill.

Fine views now open up across the Arun valley to Bignor Hill and the western Downs. To the south, Arundel castle can be seen and, on a clear day, Chichester cathedral is also visible, standing up out of the plain.

After going through a gateway, turn left, still following a line of hawthorn trees on your left. In about 200 yards, bear slightly away from the hedge, following a rutted track, and go through a metal field gate. Now go ahead across a small area of rough pasture and enter woodland on a clear track. Follow this track along the hillside within the woodland, unfenced at first and subsequently with a fence to the left only. After a mile you will reach a meeting of five ways.

Near here stood Jack Upperton's Gibbet. Jack Upperton, perpetrator of an 18th century mail robbery, was hanged at the scene of the crime on the road which used to cross the Downs from Storrington, passing this point.

At the junction of five ways, turn sharply back to the left through a Forestry Commission gate and immediately fork right, now heading south-east, on a forestry track which takes you out, after a little over ½ mile, through a wooden barrier on to a flint and gravel track where you should turn right.

In ¼ mile, opposite 'Flint Cottage', fork left, still on a wide track. After another 300 yards, at a junction with a metalled drive, go straight ahead on a narrow woodland path which skirts to the left of a small car parking area. On the other side of the wood turn right on a metalled road and, in 180 yards, just before reaching a wooden bungalow on the left, turn left on a wide track between fences. After 150 yards, turn right and follow a fence out to the main A27 road. Turn left along the road for a few yards to regain the car parking area.

HIGHDOWN HILL AND CLAPHAM

WALK 15

★

3½ or 6 miles (5.5 or 9.5 km)

OS Landranger sheets 197 and 198

Highdown Hill, at the start of this walk, stands isolated from the main downland area, closely overlooking Worthing and the coastal plain, with views extending, on a clear day, from the Isle fo Wight to Beachy Head. It is the site of an Iron Age fort, the ramparts of which enclose a pagan Saxon cemetery. Both have been excavated and the finds are in Worthing museum.

From the open National Trust area on the top of Highdown, the walk drops to Patching Pond and then climbs, giving a good idea of the way in which the southern dip slope of the Downs ascends gently towards the escarpment.

Clapham is a pleasant well-kept village, now mostly modern, but with a simple 12th to 13th century church remarkable for its woodland setting. A few years ago it had a resident sheep to keep the churchyard grass down. Inside the church are some 16th century brasses commemorating three members of the Shelley family, ancestors of the poet. Clapham Farm, a solid timber-framed farmhouse adjoining the church, looks sturdily traditional.

The longer walk makes a circuit of Clapham Woods, one of the most attractive of many such patches of woodland on the southern slopes of the Downs west of this point. The walk may be extended still further by linking it with Walk 14 as detailed in the route description and indicated on the sketch map. This will give a combined length of 13½ miles.

Park at the Worthing Borough Council car park at Highdown House on Highdown Hill. To get there, turn right (north) off the A259 Worthing-Littlehampton road about ¼ mile west of the roundabout to the north of Goring on to an access road, signposted Highdown House. The car park is at the top of the hill at OS map ref. 098041.

From the car park start out half left across the open grassy hilltop aiming towards the summit of Highdown Hill. Pass through a gate in a low flint wall near a memorial enclosed by iron railings. The earthworks and a scattered group of trees are now visible ahead on the top of the hill. After passing through the ramparts and keeping to the left of a triangulation point, keep ahead westwards, now going slightly downhill, walking parallel to a hedge on your right. Immediately short of a gate and stile, take a winding path to the right through an area of scrub. Go over a stile and keep down the left hand edge of two fields, at first with a hedge and then a barbed wire fence on your left. At the bottom of the slope go over a footbridge and two more stiles and then skirt to the right of a fenced sewage area to join the main A280 road.

Turn right along this busy road for 350 yards to its junction with the even busier A27. Go straight across the A27 and take a grassy path to the right of the Horse and Groom public house and outbuildings, with Patching Pond on your right. Go over a stile and keep ahead with a hedge to the left and the pond a little way away to the right. On reaching a stile in the hedge on the left, *don't* go over it but instead bear away from the hedge diagonally to the right and slightly downhill to cross another stile and then climb in the same direction for 60 yards to a third stile giving access to a cricket ground. Cross the cricket ground and join a road immediately to the right of the village hall. Turn left along the road for about 160 yards and then, about 30 yards before reaching a right turn to Clapham village, turn right on a narrow metalled driveway lined on the right by a row of lime trees.

(To link with Walk 14 continue on up the main road for 200 yards before turning left on a narrow road, signposted Patching Street. Follow this for a little over ¼ mile and then turn right at a T-junction on the cul-de-sac to Patching church. Fork left along the rough track towards the church and in a few yards bear left through farm buildings. Immediately beyond the buildings bear round to the right on a flint track between fences. You are now on Walk 14.)

To continue with Walk 15 follow the driveway lined with lime trees which soon becomes a narrow path between fences and leads out to a track opposite a house called Summerfold. For the shorter walk of 3½ miles turn right here and skip the next three paragraphs of description, but if you have time it is worth following the longer walk at least as far as the lovely little church of Clapham.

To follow the longer 6 mile walk, turn left at Summerfold and follow the track out to a road. Go straight across this road and ahead along another road, soon keeping straight on along a rough track between fences and over a crossing track to reach Clapham church. Go through the churchyard, keeping round to the left of the church and leaving the churchyard over a stile. Cross a short open field and go over another stile into Clapham Woods. On reaching a cleared area, go straight over an oblique crossing track and follow the track ahead which soon re-enters the woods. At a T-junction go right, skirting to the left of another cleared area. At the next Y-junction, go left with the main track, ignoring a left fork after a few more yards. In another 200 yards, ignore a right fork, always keeping on the main track which now levels out with views glimpsed through woods to the left.

Go straight across another small open area, completely surrounded by woods, and continue on a clear woodland track, now with a fence and a steep slope dropping away to your left. After leaving the woods over a stile, go ahead on a grassy track between fields for about 150 yards before doubling back to the right on a clear trackway between fences to re-enter Clapham Woods. Now descend, ignoring all side and crossing tracks.

After leaving the woods, pass Keeper's Cottage (right) and about 200 yards after passing another cottage (left), turn right on a narrow path which follows a fence line westwards, first to the north of the fence and then to the south of it. In ½ mile the path leads you out to a T-junction with a rough track. Turn left and in a few yards, right, along a road which leads you back into Clapham village. In about 200 yards you will be able to recognize and turn left along the track by which you came into the village.

(The description of the shorter walk resumes here.)

Follow this track southwards through a field gate and down the left hand edge of a field. After passing some farm buildings on the left, go straight ahead through two gates and uphill with a fence and a derelict brickfield to the right. Continue on a track through open woodland. Within sight and sound of the A27 ahead, turn right on a crossing track which skirts the perimeter of an industrial area. Look out for a narrow path to the left with a 'no cycling' notice at the start of it and follow it out to the A27.

Go straight across the main road and turn right along it, using the pavement on the opposite side. In 100 yards turn left on a wide track, partly metalled. Go straight over a crossing track, then across an open area before climbing through woodland on to Highdown Hill, all on a clear track. At a National Trust notice bear left across the shoulder of the hill and so back to the car park.

To Findon

|||||||||||||||||||
WALK 16
|||||||||||||||||||

Corrugated Iron
Barn

Cissbury Ring

To Steyning

To Walk 19

Lychpole Hill

To Sompting

Steep Down

N

Flint Barn

To Steyning

Pumping Station

SOMPTING

Ch

Park Here (**Start**)

A27
To Lancing

A27
To Worthing

CISSBURY RING

WALK 16

★

6½ or 7½ miles (10.5 or 12 km)

OS Landranger sheet 198

Starting from the edge of the coastal plain, this walk climbs quickly into bare and lonely downland, the slopes a patchwork of intense cultivation. Although of a fair length, it is mostly very easy going, much of it on broad, well used tracks. At least two of these are probably ancient, since they are among the half dozen rights of way which radiate from Cissbury.

Cissbury Ring, the largest and most spectacular prehistoric camp on the South Downs, was known simply as Bury until the 16th century (from the old English *burh*, a stronghold). Although time has rounded the steep ramparts and partly filled in the ditches, it remains an impressive place. It has been calculated that 60,000 tons of chalk were moved in its making, and it has a long history. Originally a Neolithic camp, it was the scene of extensive flint mining, of which the only traces today are a number of depressions in the ground at the south-west end. Carbon dating of antler picks found in the excavated mine shafts suggest that this was about 2700 BC. Two Neolithic skeletons were also found. Later it became an Iron Age fort, probably containing a sizeable community. It was farmed during the Roman period and then refortified against Saxon raiders. Looking north-east from Cissbury it is possible to detect the faint shadows of lynchets lying across some of the cornfields, a relic of very ancient cultivation, probably connected with Cissbury.

It is interesting to note that the track which the walk takes eastwards from Cissbury is an example of what is officially designated as a 'Road used as a Public Path'. This label is often a hint of antiquity and this particular road can be traced on the map running directly both westwards to the Arun and eastwards to the Adur at Coombes, where it could have linked with the Ridgeway at Botolphs. It is tempting to speculate that this might have been the track used for exporting the flints from the Cissbury mines to other parts of southern England.

This walk can be linked with Walk 19 to give a combined circuit of 12½ miles. The link is indicated in the route description.

Park at Sompting church (OS map ref. 162055). To get there turn left (north) off the A27 Worthing-Brighton road on to the unclassified road to Steyning which leaves the main road about a mile west of Lancing and which is signposted to Sompting Parish Church. Park on the left of the road where it is at its widest, about 100 to 150 yards north of the junction with the A27. NB. It is not possible to turn right from the A27 into the Sompting-Steyning road.

Take a path to the left (westwards) off the Sompting-Steyning road, which leaves the road about 100 yards south of the church, opposite the entrance to Thornbury House. After 200 yards, turn right along another narrow path between fence and hedge which climbs on to the Downs. This soon becomes a wider track up the right hand edge of a field with a fence to the right. In 300 yards turn left along the top edge of this field still with a fence to the right. Ahead and slightly left you can see Highdown Hill which is the start and finish of Walk 15.

At the end of the field go right, now once again between fence and hedge. After passing through a bridle gate, keep straight on along a wide track with a belt of woodland on your left, soon keeping right with a more substantial track. Immediately after passing a flint barn on the right, keep left on the higher of two approximately parallel trackways round the base of Lychpole Hill. In a little over 400 yards, go through the leftmost of two field gates and immediately turn left at a Y-junction and bear right on a well ridden track with a fence to the right and the scrub-covered side of Lychpole Hill up to the left.

In nearly a mile, after passing through a bridle gate, go forward for about 50 yards before forking left past a National Trust notice 'Cissbury Ring' uphill through fairly dense scrub. Towards the top of the hill, bear right on a crossing track which drops gradually downhill for about 1/4 mile to the Cissbury Ring parking area.

From this point I can strongly recommend the walker to climb the clear track up on to Cissbury and to make a circuit of the outer ramparts, adding a mile to the total distance.

To continue with the rest of the walk, return to the car parking area and leave it by a clear chalk and flint track which doubles back to the right from the track by which you reached the car park before climbing on to Cissbury. Drop down into a valley in an easterly direction with a fence on your left and walking on a lower level than and roughly parallel to the track by which you approached Cissbury. In 1/4 mile keep left by a corrugated iron barn, straight on along the lower of two tracks.

Follow the main track now for about 1 1/2 miles, ignoring side and cross tracks and going straight across the Sompting-Steyning road. About 1/4 mile beyond the road turn right on a fenced track which follows a line of electricity pylons southward along the western flank of Steep Down. (To link with Walk 19 keep straight on instead of turning right and in a little more than 100 yards, turn right and climb on to Steep Down as described in Walk 19.)

Follow the track and the pylons southwards for 1 1/2 miles, passing a water pumping station and some derelict farm buildings on the left, to reach the main A27 dual carriageway. Turn right and follow the path on the near (north) side of the main road. In just over 100 yards, bear right on a grassy path with a hedge on your right. In about 50 yards go through a swing gate and follow the right hand edge of a field, diverging gradually from the A27, with woodland on your right. (The path winding into woodland just before the swing gate is not a right of way.) In the far right hand corner of the field, go through a gate which brings you out on the road within yards of the start of the walk.

CHANCTONBURY RING AND WASHINGTON

WALK 17

★

4½ miles (7 km)

OS Landranger sheet 198

The main feature of this relatively short walk is Chanctonbury Ring, which must surely be the most famous landmark on the South Downs. The gentle climb up to the Ring follows one of the most attractive bostal (see p. 76) routes on the northern escarpment. After a fine stretch of the South Downs Way and a descent to the village of Washington, the circuit is completed through fields at the foot of the Downs and along the bottom of a hanger which covers the northern slope of the Downs below Chanctonbury Ring.

Chanctonbury Ring is the site of an Iron Age hill fort of which the rampart is just visible. Inside it were found the remains of a Romano-Celtic temple. Quite a few legends have become attached to it concerning encounters with the Devil at midnight on Midsummer's Eve and so forth, but more interesting is the clump of beech trees which has made it such a striking and immediately recognizable landmark. They were planted by Charles Goring of Wiston in 1760, when he was a schoolboy, and lovingly tended and watered by him with the 'almost hopeless wish' that he would see them properly established. He lived to 85 and his wish was granted. The sight of the clump, epitome of the Downs for so many, must have given pleasure to many thousands of lovers of Sussex ever since. Sadly the Great Gale of October 1987 has reduced the clump to a sparse remnant, but strenuous replanting efforts are in hand. The hill is 800 feet up and offers views of almost the whole of Sussex, as well as a stretch of the Surrey hills and glimpses of Kent and Hampshire.

Washington stands at the northern end of an ancient river valley through the Downs from which the river vanished millions of years ago, leaving the so-called 'wind-gap' used by the A24 road.

Park at the car park and picnic area at the foot of Chanctonbury Hill. To reach it, turn left (south) off the A283 Steyning-Storrington road on to a narrow unclassified road (signposted to Chanctonbury) at OS map ref. 144135, about 2½ miles north-west of Steyning. The car park and picnic area are on the left in about ¾ mile, almost at the foot of the Downs (OS map ref. 146124).

Continue southwards along the road by which you arrived. This soon becomes a rough chalk and flint track and you should follow this as it

keeps to the right of an old quarry and then curves to the left above it.
There are various unofficial short cuts straight up the wooded slope to
Chanctonbury Ring, but the right of way follows the main track on a
more gentle ascent through woodland and out on to the open downland
at the top. On reaching the wide South Downs Way crossing track, turn
right and follow it up to Chanctonbury Ring.

Continue westwards with the South Downs Way. In about 600 yards,
just beyond a crossing fence line, look out for a dewpond on the right
of the track. Dewponds, which are such a feature of the Downs, are,
in spite of their picturesque name, shallow depressions lined with clay
(or sometimes concrete nowadays) which collect rainwater rather than
dew. Before the days of piped water supplies they were a vital source
of water for the huge flocks of sheep which used to crop the dry chalk
downland. Nowadays they are often leaky, dry and grass-grown. This
example, one of the highest on the Downs, was restored by the Society
of Sussex Downsmen in 1971.

Keep on along the South Downs Way from which there are good
views of Cissbury Ring (Walk 16) away to the south. About ¼ mile
beyond the dewpond, turn right, still with the South Downs Way, and
follow it downhill passing a gas pressure-reducing station on the right.
A few years ago this was quite an eyesore, but careful landscaping with
indigenous trees has made it much less intrusive. After another 200
yards, turn right off the South Downs Way on a clear grassy track
which, after about 150 yards, narrows and drops down with a chalk
quarry to the left. Descend through woodland and over a stile, finally
crossing an open field to a road.

Turn right along the road for about 200 yards and about 200 yards
short of the Frankland Arms public house, turn right over a stile and
keep along the left hand edge of the first field before climbing steeply
up a flight of steps with a wooden handrail. Go ahead over two more
stiles and then keep along the left hand edge of a large field, passing

some farm buildings on the left and walking parallel to the wooded slopes of the Downs away to the right.

About 400 yards beyond the farm buildings, bear right on a narrow track, usually well trodden out across arable land, aiming for Chanctonbury Ring which can be seen on top of the hill ahead, and crossing two fields.

After reaching the woodland at the foot of the Downs escarpment, fork left and follow a track within the edge of the trees. Keep to this bridleway along the foot of the Downs for ¾ mile, finally turning left on a metalled road for a few yards to regain the car park.

STEYNING ROUND HILL

WALK 18

★

4½ miles (7 km)

OS Landranger sheet 198

Starting from Steyning, and very much a Steyning walk throughout, the route overlooks the town from a number of viewpoints, notably Steyning Round Hill which Arthur Mee calls 'a great natural amphitheatre, one of the marvellous hill tops of Sussex.'

Seen from the hills Steyning is a pleasant modern town, spreading a little up the foot of the hill, but controlled and well cared for. Right at the heart of this modern brick and tile there is, however, a great richness of old building. The general impression of the central area is of a Georgian market town, as exemplified by the charming tile-hung Market House with its little clock turret in the High Street, but there are quite a few much older buildings. In Church Street (soon after the walk begins) there are some fine 15th century buildings which were converted into a Grammar School founded in 1614. The school has a handsome brick porch. The tall flint house with the overhanging close-timbered gable in the High Street opposite Church Street was originally the gaol.

Steyning church is famous for its magnificent Norman nave, splendidly arched and richly carved, lofty and clearly lit by rows of high clerestory windows. This is all that remains of the Norman church built in the 12th century on the site of an earlier church founded by St. Cuthman.

In the days when it could be reached by small sea-going ships sailing up the estuary which almost covered the Adur valley, Steyning was known as St. Cuthman's Port. During the reign of William the Conqueror, all ships passing Bramber castle had to pay a toll of two pence to the Lord of Bramber. Exactly where the ships unloaded is uncertain — somewhere north-east of the church has been suggested. There was a deposit of shingle there at one time and during the flooding of 1924 a wide creek appeared nearby.

Park at the long-stay car park in Steyning village at OS map ref. 179113. Turn north off the A283 in the middle of the village into Church Street. The entrance to the car park is on the right in about 350 yards, opposite Steyning church.

Leave the car park by the far (southern) end away from the entrance, and turn right on a narrow tarmac path which takes you out into a lane (School Lane). At a T-junction by the Norfolk Arms public house, turn left into Church Street and follow it past the old buildings of Steyning Grammar School on the left to the High Street where turn right. Follow the main street for a little over 300 yards, and then, a few yards after Tanyard Lane turns off to the right, you should turn left on a narrow path with a central metal handrail. This takes you through to another lane where you turn right. Follow the lane round to the left and, immediately after passing the SME factory on the right, keep straight ahead on a rough track which aims for the foot of the Downs.

After passing some allotments on the left the path narrows and climbs between hedges. In a little over ½ mile, at a rifle range boundary notice and flagpole, turn left and follow a clear path (known locally as the lower horseshoe) round the lower slope of Pepperscombe, keeping approximately on the 300 foot contour line and near to the lower edge of woodland and scrub on the steep side of the combe. In two places the path divides to give parallel alternative routes. Either will do, but in each case the right of way keeps to the lower path. After very nearly a mile, about 60 yards short of a road, turn sharply back to the right on a wide track which climbs fairly steeply, soon with quarry workings to the left. Towards the top of the quarry, fork left on the steeper and more eroded of two tracks.

Looking back from this point there is a good view over Steyning and across the Adur valley to the profiles of Truleigh Hill in the foreground, with Newtimber Hill and Wolstonbury Hill beyond.

Now follow a fine terraced track which climbs and skirts round the top of Pepperscombe (the so-called upper horseshoe path). Pass to the right of a wooden seat and continue on a narrow but well trodden path which keeps along the upper edge of woodland and scrub on the side of the combe giving a succession of views out across the Weald. After a good ½ mile, when you are squarely above the head of the combe, fork right and slightly downhill on the clearer of two fairly narrow tracks with the steep slope of the combe dropping away fairly sharply to the right of the path. Soon there is a steep slope also up to the left of the path, which now follows a terraceway.

Soon after coming out on a more open section of track with Steyning church and Wolstonbury Beacon in direct line ahead, fork left on a path which soon re-enters woodland which has been badly devastated by the 1987 gale. At a T-junction keep right and continue to descend. Keep with the main track which fairly soon bears right and follows down the right hand edge of a large field.

About 40 yards short of the metalled lane at the bottom turn right up a bank and walk along a fence line. In about 50 yards go over a stile and cross a pasture field on a path which aims straight for Steyning church and is usually well trodden out. At the other end of the field go over another stile, cross a driveway and keep to the right of a wooden hut to cross a footbridge and follow a narrow path between fence and wall out to a lane.

Turn left on the lane for 30 yards only before going right on another narrow path between gardens. This leads you out to another lane by the SME factory. From this point you can retrace your outgoing route to the car park.

COOMBES AND STEEP DOWN

WALK 19

★

6 miles (10 km)

OS Landranger sheet 198

This is a fairly easy but exhilarating walk, up and down across open cultivated downland to the west of the Adur valley. It offers a succession of magnificent views and goes through the interesting hamlet of Coombes. The path drops down into Coombes through a wood on the side of a combe which probably gave it its name. All that remains of the village are a few houses and a farm clustered round a tiny Saxon church of grey knapped flints, with a roof of Horsham stone and a little red-tiled belfry. It is primitive, unrestored, atmospheric and endearing. The chancel arch is no more than a simple rounded doorway. The faded and rather fragmentary wall paintings were discovered in 1949 and are thought to be pre-12th century. There are signs that a bank originally enclosed the churchyard, suggesting that the church was built on a pre-Christian religious site.

A link with Walk 16 is indicated in the route description, a combined circuit of 12½ miles.

Park on the edge of the Downs to the north of North Lancing. The car parking area can be reached by turning right (north), signposted North Lancing, at the roundabout on the A27 Shoreham-Worthing road about 2 miles west of the River Adur (OS map ref. 186055). In 300 yards turn right into Mill Road and climb to the Downs, finally forking left on a rough track. The car park is to the left of this track in about 100 yards (OS map ref. 184062).

Start the walk by going over the track by which you approached the Downs. Cross a rough grassy area to join a track which skirts to the left of an old quarry area. In a few yards only, turn left over a stile and go straight across the first field, aiming for another stile. Follow a clear track across the next field over a low summit, soon aiming for the chimney of Shoreham cement works which can be seen across the Adur valley. Go over another stile and drop down into a valley on a path between fences. At the bottom, pass to the right of a flint-walled enclosure and climb again, soon with a line of trees to your right. Beyond the trees, where the track curves to the right through a metal gate, keep straight ahead over a stile, then across a concrete track and over another stile. Keep up along the right hand edge of the next field with a line of trees once again on your right as you go over a summit. Ignore a track which goes back to the right and keep ahead, now with a fence line to your right. Go over another stile and keep along the left hand edge of the next field as you go over another summit. In about 200 yards, at the field corner, turn right. Ignore a signed bridleway which doubles back to the left. After a few more yards, turn sharply left on a narrow path which descends through woodland to the beautiful downland church of Coombes.

After leaving the churchyard, descend across a paddock and out on to a farm track which leads you out through the handful of houses which make up the hamlet of Coombes to a road.

Turn left along the road for about ¼ mile. Although unclassified it can be rather busy at weekends, but there is a reasonable verge for most of the distance. As the road passes under power lines, turn left through a gap and drop down a steep grassy bank and on through an area of scrub. At the bottom, go through a gate, and keep along the left hand edge of a field for ⅓ mile with a hedge on your left. Follow this hedge line through a gate and past a white-walled cottage on the left. About 150 yards after passing the cottage turn left through a bridle gate and climb through a narrow strip of woodland to a T-junction with a broad track. Turn left along this track and follow it round to the right past the entrance to the cottage called Tinpots.

The odd name of the cottage has been linked with the fact that this was the ancient route by which tin was conveyed from Cornwall to the seaport of Pevensey. There may have been a Roman bridge across the river nearby.

About 120 yards after you have curved to the right by Tinpots, now on the South Downs Way, go through a metal gate and follow a clear track up on to Annington Hill. From this path there are views of Bramber with its prominent castle ruin, away to the right. Beyond another field gate, the South Downs Way has (so far unofficially) been diverted down the hill to the right and round the right hand edge of a large field. Follow the edge of the field round and up to the Steyning-Sompting road on the top of the hill.

Turn left along the road for 100 yards only before forking left on a clear track. Follow this for ½ mile to the foot of Steep Down where you go over a crossing track, under power lines and through a gateway before turning right and climbing fairly steeply with a fence on your right to the triangulation point on the top of Steep Down. (To link with Walk 16, turn right on the crossing track at the foot of Steep Down.)

From the summit there are extensive views in all directions. All round to the north there is a great expanse of bare rolling downland and a segment of the Weald beyond. To the south-east there are views across the Adur, where it widens on its approach to Shoreham harbour, to the distant chalk cliffs beyond Brighton. To the south-west, beyond the coastal plain, you might catch a glimpse of the Isle of Wight and westwards, not far away, the crest of Cissbury (Walk 16) is visible.

From the triangulation point bear left along the ridge of Steep Down, heading south-east towards the clump of trees on the next hill, known as Lancing Ring. At the bottom of the hill, at a T-junction, turn left and in a little more than 50 yards turn sharply right. Climb on a clear track which passes to the left of Lancing Ring and descends, taking you straight back to the car park.

FULKING AND THE DEVIL'S DYKE

WALK 20

★

4½ miles (7 km)

OS Landranger sheet 198

This walk begins by turning away from the Downs and following some less well trodden paths across Wealden farmland. After a sharp climb to the hills from Poynings it skirts the rim of the Devil's Dyke, the most striking combe on the South Downs. The rest is easy going along the ridgeway with a final descent to the Shepherd and Dog at Fulking, where the walk begins and ends.

Fulking, a village rather unusually without a church, is situated at the foot of one of the most dramatic escarpments in the entire length of the Downs. It is also the most characteristic of all the downland spring-line villages. The spring, which never fails (it kept going even during the catastrophic drought of 1976), gushes out of the steep hillside in a copse just above the Shepherd and Dog and runs down to the roadside. Esther Meynell, in her book on Sussex published in 1947, relates that in the old days of sheep-rearing on the Downs the stream used to be dammed in this hollow and a sheepwash made in the bend of the lane. The pub probably gets its name from this.

Poynings, another spring-line village tucked against the foot of the scarp slope, has a very fine cruciform church with a massive, battlemented square tower. The interior is beautifully light and lofty. It has often been compared with the church at Alfriston (Walk 27).

The Devil's Dyke has always been popular. In the Railway Age it was thought worth building a branch line from the coast to bring tourists almost to the top of the hill. The railway has gone but the Dyke still attracts thousands of visitors, though most of them do not usually stray far from the car park. This walk keeps just far enough away from the cars to avoid most of the crowds.

Park at Fulking which is situated on the unclassified road running along the foot of the Downs linking the A281 Pyecombe-Henfield road with the A2037 Upper Beeding-Henfield road. It is possible to park at several places on the roadside verge immediately to the west of the village. The ideal spot, if there is room, is immediately west of the Shepherd and Dog public house, near a roadside stream (OS map ref. 246113).

Start off by walking back into the village from the Shepherd and Dog. In a little over 100 yards, about 50 yards before reaching a shop on the left, turn left through a gate which takes you into a recreation ground. Keep along the right hand edge of this open grassy area, over wooden railings and then diagonally right across an open field. At the far right hand corner of this field go through a gap over a culvert and keep along the right hand edge of the next field, now in an easterly direction. At the first field corner go ahead over a stile and immediately turn left and follow the left hand edge of a field, now heading north. Follow the headland northwards for ¼ mile on a stiled path. Keep along the left hand edge of a paddock and, where the hedge veers away to the left, go ahead to find and cross a stile and a plank bridge over a stream. Immediately beyond the stream, turn right and walk parallel to the stream on your right. A stiled path takes you across a meadow and through a rather damp and overgrown area to reach a road.

Turn right along the road for about 250 yards, and then go left through a rather dilapidated bridle gate converted into a stile beside a metal field gate. Go slightly left and uphill to the corner of a copse and then follow the left hand edge of the field with woodland to the left, now in an easterly direction and parallel to the Downs. Keep going east over an open field along the top of a low ridge. Newtimber Hill, with its wooded summit, is directly ahead. In the next field, bear slightly left and down hill, and after crossing the corner of a third field, go over a footbridge by a clump of trees. Continue eastwards over a stile and forward, soon on a more substantial track out to a road.

Turn right along the road for 60 yards and then go left on a metalled track through a school playground, passing to the left of a school hall. Go over a stile and continue along the left hand edge of a field. In the next field corner, cross a stile and stream and head across the next field aiming for a field gate with Newtimber Hill still directly ahead.

Do not go through the field gate but turn right just short of it and follow the left hand edge of a field with a fence and low bank to the left, aiming now for some farm buildings which can be seen ahead, a little to the left of Poynings church. On approaching the farm, veer slightly right, away from the fence line, and head towards a Dutch barn with the church beyond. Go through the farmyard and out to a road opposite the church.

Turn right along the road, and in 50 yards, at a T-junction, turn left. Now, to avoid walking on the road, take a parallel path which starts through a stone archway on the right of the road. About 100 yards after passing the Royal Oak public house on the right, and almost opposite the entrance to Dyke Farm House, turn left on a metalled driveway (Dyke Lane) which soon becomes a rough track between fence and hedge. At the foot of the steep wooded slope of the Downs, where the path divides into three, take the left hand track and follow it up through woodland and out on to scrub-covered hillside. As the path levels out it follows the edge of the Devil's Dyke which drops steeply away to the left. Ignore cross tracks and follow the main track out to a road.

Turn left along the near side verge, with a magnificent view to your left along the whole length of the Devil's Dyke. Shortly, turn right through a bridle gate and go ahead across open downland to reach the edge of the northern escarpment with a tremendous view over the Weald. Go forward along the edge of the scarp slope. In about $1/2$ mile, where the track descends into a dip, double back sharply to the right, downhill, on a track hollowed out quite deeply between banks. About halfway down the hill, double back sharply to the left on a crossing track and follow it downhill through a belt of scrub. Go over a stile in the perimeter fence of the recently acquired National Trust Fulking escarpment area. Bear right for 5 yards and walk down along the left hand edge of a field towards the buildings of Fulking village. About two-thirds of the way along the field, go left and descend through the car park of the Shepherd and Dog public house and so back to the start of the walk.

WOLSTONBURY AND NEWTIMBER

WALK 21

★

5½ miles (9 km)

OS Landranger sheet 198

You will have to contend with several ups and downs on this walk but the ups are in each case a good deal less steep than the downs., You will encounter scarp, beech woods, open grassy hilltops, chalk pits, tiny churches, Iron Age ramparts and immense views of Downs and Weald — the downland in microcosm and a splendid introduction to this unique landscape.

Wolstonbury Hill, 670 feet high, stands clear of the line of the Downs and is a landmark for miles. Its crest is encircled by the ramparts of an Iron Age fort. The views are superb — Ashdown Forest to the north-east, the Surrey Hills and Blackdown to the north-west.

The Devil's Dyke, seen from afar and to good effect from Newtimber Hill on this walk, is a steep-sided combe eroded in the escarpment. Some geologists think it might have been excavated during the Ice Age by water flowing from a thawing ice cap, but, if so, the debris has inexplicably vanished. An earlier theory ascribes it to the Devil, who, annoyed by the number of churches in the Weald, tried one night to cut a dyke through the Downs to let in the sea and drown the Christians. Mistaking an old woman's candle at a cottage window for the dawn, he hurriedly abandoned the task.

The church at Newtimber is mostly a Victorian restoration, but attractively set in the valley between the hills of Wolstonbury and Newtimber, among the trees and the few houses which are all that survive of the village. These include Newtimber Place, a moated 17th century manor which is occasionally open to the public. 238 acres of Newtimber Hill are owned by the National Trust who have cut a number of paths through the woods on the northern slope, one of which is used on this walk.

Pyecombe is a scattered village on the A23. It has a little flint church, partly Norman, with an unusual lead font, 12th century and beautifully ornamented. The village was famous years ago for the making of shepherds' crooks.

Park at New Way Lane under Wolstonbury Hill. New Way Lane is a turning westwards off the A273 Pyecombe-Burgess Hill road at Clayton, immediately to the south of the Jack and Jill public house at OS map ref. 299142. Follow the lane westwards for about ¾ mile and park on the grass verge a few yards after the lane turns north at OS map ref. 289143.

Start the walk on a path which continues westwards where New Way Lane turns sharply north. In about 250 yards turn left (south) with a clear track and enter the beechwoods at the foot of Wolstonbury Hill. After entering the woods, go right on a crossing track and, in a few yards, fork left over a stile and, immediately, keep right on a path which climbs obliquely out of the woodland. Follow this fine terraced path up round the shoulder of the hill, with views ahead to Chanctonbury Ring and the western Downs. Shortly after crossing a stile in a fence line you should fork left on a less well defined path which continues ahead along the grassy hillside with old quarry workings away up the hill to the left. Aim towards the wooded slopes of Newtimber Hill which can be seen ahead across the valley. After passing through an area of scattered scrub, go through a weighted bridle gate and immediately turn left on a crossing track for 5 yards only before turning right over a stile. Now drop steeply downhill with a barbed wire fence to your right, aiming just to the left of more modern quarry workings in the valley. The path skirts closely to the left of the quarry with the steep hillside rising on the left. Immediately beyond the quarry, go over a stile in the fence line to the right and follow a clear chalky track past some buildings. Go ahead to pass under the new A23 dual carriageway.

Immediately beyond the underpass, turn right along the slip road and within a few yards, break away to the left to cross a stile in the roadside fence. Walk along the left hand edge of a field. At the corner of this field go over a stile and keep along the right hand edge of the next field to Newtimber church. Go over a stile into the churchyard, follow the main church path out to a road and turn left.

Follow this road for a little over ¼ mile and then go straight across the main A281 Brighton-Horsham road into Beggars Lane, passing a National Trust notice 'Newtimber Hill' on the right. In about 200 yards take a National Trust footpath to the left which climbs up some steps on to the side of Newtimber Hill. In about 150 yards, where the path forks, take the lower left hand path signposted 'woodland' which traverses the wooded hillside, climbing gently at first. Descend, ignoring a path to the right, to reach a T-junction with a bridleway where you should turn right.

Follow this clear track which curves to the left and climbs to the top of Newtimber Hill. Ignore side tracks, and after passing through a bridle gate near the top, keep straight ahead up and out on to the open grassy summit continuing over pasture (there is no defined path) in a south-easterly direction, walking approximately parallel to a thin line of trees some distance away to the left, beyond which can be seen the twin windmills known as Jack and Jill. Converge gradually on the hedge line to the left of the open area. As you cross the summit there are good views of the deep rift of the Devil's Dyke across the valley to the right.

Follow the hedge line to the far left corner of the open grassy National Trust area and here turn left through a bridle gate and follow the left hand edge of a field in an easterly direction, now on the South Downs Way. In ¼ mile, bear left and drop down on a wide chalky track.

On reaching the A23, divert to the left with the South Downs Way to cross a new bridge over the main road. A few yards beyond the bridge, turn right and walk up to Pyecombe church. Immediately past the church, turn left along a road called 'The Wyshe' which soon narrows to a path and climbs steadily. Follow this path for ½ mile to a wide crossing track where you should turn left through a bridle gate to the right of a field gate. After a further ½ mile and about 150 yards after passing through a bridle gate, turn right on a green strip across an open field, aiming for the summit of Wolstonbury Hill. After crossing a stile climb to the triangulation point on the top.

From here, drop down the steep north slope of the hill, aiming towards the farm and mansion of the Danny estate in the valley below. The path is not very well defined at first as it winds through the Iron Age earthworks but is much clearer on the steep slope. Towards the bottom of the hill go through a belt of woodland to rejoin your outgoing route and retrace your footsteps to the car parking area.

DITCHLING BEACON AND EAST CHILTINGTON

WALK 22

★

6½ miles (10.5 km)

OS Landranger sheet 198

Ditchling Beacon, at 813 feet, is one of the three highest points on the South Downs, with magnificent views across the Weald towards Blackdown in the west, Ashdown Forest to the north-east, and in between them the Surrey hills and, on a clear day, the white chalk pits of the North Downs.

The walk, starting high up on the chalk, drops quickly into the Weald and follows a sandy ridge eastwards from Streat, with fine views of the long bare skyline of the Downs, before climbing up on to the chalk again via Plumpton Bostal. During the last 1½ miles along the ancient ridgeway followed by the South Downs Way, it is interesting to look down on the Weald and pick out the route of the first part of the walk, clearly marked by the little churches at Westmeston, Streat, East Chiltington and Plumpton.

Park in the car park at the top of Ditchling Beacon (OS map ref. 333130). This can be reached by taking the Ditchling road north out of Brighton, crossing the new bypass at Old Boat corner (OS map ref. 325095) and continuing northwards to the top of the Downs. Alternatively you can take the steep and winding road which climbs to the top of the beacon from Ditchling village.

Cross the road from the car park and start off eastwards along the South Downs Way. In a few yards only, however, drop down to the left over a stile and obliquely down the escarpment on a clear path. In an area of old quarry workings near the bottom of the hill, turn left on a wider track and follow it down through a gate and on within a line of trees and past farm buildings to the road at Westmeston.

Westmeston is one of many spring-line villages dotted along the foot of the northern scarp of the Downs where water rises out of the base of the chalk. It has a characteristic downland church which has been much restored but still has its 14th century timber porch.

Turn right along the main road, passing the church on your left (there is a wide grass verge), and a little over 100 yards beyond the church go left over a stile and half right across a field, looking out for another stile in the hedge to your right which takes you into an enclosed track between hedge and metal fence. This leads out to a broad gravel track where you should turn left. Now follow this clear track northwards for almost a mile ignoring side paths and one wide crossing track. On reaching the buildings of Hayleigh Farm turn right between some fuel storage tanks to find steps and a stile. Beyond the stile the line of the path is diagonally half left uphill across the open field. In the top corner of the field join a broad track at a stile.

At this point and at various stages during the next 1½ miles there are fine views across to the Downs. The 'V' of trees visible on the scarp slope was planted in commemoration of Queen Victoria's jubilee in 1887.

Turn right along the track and follow it past Streat church to a road where turn left. Streat is beautifully situated on a sandy ridge running east to west. The name derives from the Roman road which followed this ridge on its way to join Stane Street in the Arun valley (see Walk 9).

Having turned left, follow the road for 60 yards and then, opposite a letter-box in a brick pillar, turn right on a wide track. Continue eastwards on this track for nearly a mile, finally on a metalled section along the southern perimeter of Plumpton Race Course. This part is actually on the line of the Roman road. Just beyond the race course go straight across a road and continue almost straight ahead, still on a wide track, for about ½ mile to the small 12th to 14th century church of East Chiltington.

Immediately after passing the church, turn right following the churchyard wall round and in a few yards bear away left, following the main track through a gateway with a notice beside it, 'Footpath to Plumpton Lane'. After 300 yards, fork right, passing to the right of a large pond. Follow this roughly metalled track for nearly a mile out to a road.

71

Go straight across the road and take a narrow path between hedges which starts immediately to the right of a letter-box. In a few yards go over a stile and drop down diagonally left across a field to a stream crossing. Go half right across the next field and go through a bridle gate in the corner. Keep round the left hand edge of two sides of the next field and after going through a field gate in the far left corner turn left on a dirt track. In 170 yards (under overhead wires) turn right along the near side of a hedge and ditch and in about 200 yards go left through a double metal field gate. Now strike out across the next field aiming directly towards Plumpton church — there is no visible path. At the top of the field go over a stile and cross a farm-vehicle park. Go over a stile by some meteorological instruments and keep straight ahead to cross another stile and a concrete farm road into the corner of Plumpton churchyard. Plumpton church with its attractive shingled spire is mainly 13th century.

Leave the churchyard through the main entrance and turn left on a path between hedge and wooden fence, passing the buildings of Plumpton Agricultural College. On reaching the college access road turn right and in about 100 yards, where the road curves right, go left through a bridle gate, and, after a short enclosed path, right over a stile. Now aim for the far right hand corner of a large paddock where you join the B2116 road at the Half Moon public house.

Turn left at the road and in 100 yards, opposite a road turning to Plumpton Green, turn right on a roughly metalled track, Plumpton Bostal. 'Bostal' is a Sussex dialect word for the steep paths climbing the escarpment of the South Downs. Often sunken or terraced, these tracks are usually very old, sometimes Roman, more often earlier.

Follow the bostal to the top of the Downs. On reaching the summit, turn right on the South Downs Way and follow it for $1\frac{1}{2}$ miles back to the car park.

WOODINGDEAN AND IFORD HILL

WALK 23

★

6 miles (9.5 km)

OS Landranger sheet 198

Although starting from the outskirts of Brighton, this is a walk which, for much of its length, crosses bare and surprisingly remote downland, following clear tracks through arable land and also traversing open stretches of grassland. There is a steady climb from Balsdean valley up on to the high ridge, rewarded by fine views across the Ouse Valley towards Lewes, the Weald beyond, and the dip in the land between the headlands of Mount Caburn and Firle Beacon. The Ouse Valley was at one time an estuary and sea-going ships sailed as far inland as Lewes, passing Rodmell and Iford, villages visible near the foot of the hill.

The last lap of the walk overlooks the long dry valley between Lewes and Brighton, with glimpses of Falmer church, and further away the spire of Stanmer church in the park which it now shares with Sussex University, part of which is also visible.

Park on the B2133 Falmer to Rottingdean road to the north of Woodingdean. There is space to park off the road about 100 yards north of the Sunblest bakery on the northern outskirts of Woodingdean at OS map ref. 356064.

From the car parking area start the walk eastwards from the road, immediately forking right to follow a track which runs parallel to and a little distance away from the built-up area of Woodingdean to the right. In 1/3 mile keep right at a fork and pass to the right of a radio mast. In 1/4 mile go over a crossing track and follow a path which runs close to some houses and gardens and then bears away from the houses slightly downhill. After going through a bridle gate keep to the right hand edge of the field ahead with a barbed wire fence to your right, climbing gently and soon aiming for a grassy reservoir mound which comes into sight ahead. After passing through another bridle gate and under power lines, bear slightly left, away from the fence line on your right to join a metalled access road at a bridle gate. Turn sharply left along the road and descend into a valley.

At the bottom where the road doubles back to the right, keep left through a metal gate, and, in 50 yards, where the main track curves to the left along the floor of the valley, go ahead through a bridle gate and follow a clear track which can be seen climbing up the hill out of the valley.

At the point where the path levels out, turn left and climb, heading a little to the right of a barn, the roof of which can be seen on the skyline.

After passing this barn, keep straight ahead over open downland. After passing to the right of another barn the track soon acquires a concrete surface and takes you to the edge of the escarpment. Where the concrete track turns away to the right, go ahead on a grassy path and in about 50 yards go through a bridle gate and turn left, following a barbed wire fence on your left. Follow this superb ridge path (part of the South Downs Way) along the edge of the Downs above the village of Kingston for about a mile.

Soon after passing a restored dew pond on your right, bear left over a stile between two gates, passing another pond on the left, and follow a clear track. This is Jugg's Road, the old route between Brighton and Lewes over the Downs and was used by the Brighton fishwives to bring their husbands' catch for sale in Lewes. It was originally known as 'Juggs Bostal' and was called after the nickname 'Jug' given to the Brighton fishermen.

Where the track opens out on to a wide grassy slope, the official route follows the fence on the right, though most walkers seem to use the higher path to the left. After passing through a metal field gate the South Downs Way forks to the right, but you should keep straight on along a roughly metalled track which takes you up over Newmarket Hill, past a radio mast, and back to the car park.

MOUNT CABURN

WALK 24

★

4½ miles (7 km)

OS Landranger sheet 198

Mount Caburn is a promontory at the southernmost point of a small outlier of the South Downs which is cut off from the rest of the hills by a ring of marshland and the River Ouse flowing at the foot of its cliff-like western escarpment. The walk crosses and recrosses the outlier, opening up a succession of views of the surrounding countryside — marsh, downland and Weald as well as the county town of Lewes.

For some of its length the walk is not on rights of way but follows paths licensed for public use by the Glynde Estate. Please be particularly careful to keep to the described route.

Since the first publication of this book in 1979, the rights of way on the Glynde Estate have been greatly improved and are now well waymarked. Much of the land, then under arable cultivation, has now reverted to pasture, thanks to its designation as an environmentally sensitive area whereby farmers are paid a subsidy to reduce the acreage planted with cereal crops.

Glynde is a neat and attractive village curving round the foot of Mount Caburn. For centuries it was part of the estate of Glynde Place, an Elizabethan house which is sometimes open to the public. The church, unlike most downland churches, was built in the Palladian style for the estate in 1763.

Park at Glynde. If approaching from Lewes, fork left off the A27 Lewes to Eastbourne road into Ranscombe Lane about ½ mile east of the eastern end of the Lewes bypass. On reaching a T-junction in the village, turn left and you can park almost anywhere along the wide village street. There is a particularly convenient area off the road to the right under some trees about 100 yards beyond the church and the entrance to Glynde Place (OS map ref. 456094).

Start the walk by returning down the village street and turning right into Ranscombe Lane. About 20 yards after passing the post office on the left, turn right over a stile. Go straight across the first field to another stile and then follow a well trodden path across the next field to cross a stile to the left of some trees. Go ahead up over the shoulder of the hill. At a crossing track, turn left and climb to the top of Mount Caburn.

Mount Caburn hill-fort dominates the river valley, which was an estuary until the Middle Ages. It had a long history of over five

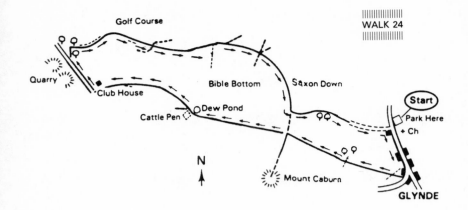

hundred years and was at first undefended. In about 100 BC a
bank and ditch were constructed, enclosing 3½ acres, and several
hundred people lived there. In addition to pottery, excavation has
revealed weaving and agricultural tackle and an Iron Age razor. A
massive outer rampart of chalk blocks with timber reinforcement was
added later, possibly as a defence against the Romans, who eventually
occupied the fort, having set fire to the timber gateway. They left
behind scabbards and sword ornaments. All the finds can be seen in
the Barbican House museum in Lewes.

From the summit, retrace your steps as far as the point where you
turned left to visit the summit. Here, turn left over a stile and head
downhill on a clear, unfenced, path across open downland. At the
bottom, cross another stile and veer left along the floor of a secluded
dry downland valley.

Go over a stile between a cattle pen and a dew pond, go ahead to
cross a second stile to the right of a gate and then veer half left across a
field, to climb obliquely up the right side of the valley towards the next
stile which soon comes into sight. Beyond the stile, turn left and, after
a few yards, fork right, signposted to Lewes, on the higher of two paths
which traverses the hillside, climbing gradually. A stiled and waymarked
path now continues along the side of the hill to reach the club house of
Lewes golf course. Follow the access road from the club house downhill,
with views over Lewes, which are seen best from the grass verge to the
left of the road, along the rim of a chalk quarry.

A few yards after the road enters trees, fork right on a wide path
and almost immediately, double back to the right up a flight of steps
and climb steeply up on to the Downs. Go over a stile and keep up the
edge of grassy downland with a line of trees to the left. Where the trees
bear away to the left, keep straight on. Your direct route across the golf
course is marked by a series of waymarked posts. Leave the golf course
over a stile and continue ahead along the side of the hill above Bible
Bottom. Cross a second stile and climb gently to a third stile on the

crest of the Ridge where a view opens out over the village of Ringmer and the Weald. Follow the ridge path, ignoring a track which forks to the left downhill.

After going over a crossing track in a dip, go slightly right over a stile by a metal gate and continue on the wide grassy ridge path over Saxon Down. About 150 yards before reaching the point where you turned left on the ridge to climb to the top of Mount Caburn on the outgoing route, turn left on a clear track which drops and keeps to the left of a clump of trees. Follow it out to the road at Glynde.

FIRLE BEACON AND THE OLD COACH ROAD

WALK 25

★

5½ miles (9 km)

OS Landranger sheets 198 and 199

This fairly easy walk would be worth doing if only for the pleasure of a two-mile stretch along the old coach road at the foot of one of the most splendid of downland escarpments, with continually changing views of the noble profile of Firle Beacon. The walk ends along the ridgeway with birds-eye views of West Firle village and the well wooded Firle Park, and goes over the top of Firle Beacon with its fifty Bronze Age barrows. The terraced bridleway by which the walk finally descends the scarp slope is probably Roman in origin.

West Firle is an unusually attractive and unspoilt downland village on the spring-line. The village spring remains to this day and was probably used by villagers only a few generations ago. The route crosses Firle Park within view of the handsome 18th century front of Firle Place in its characteristically stately-home setting. The house is on view to the public at certain times. The tower in the park was built in the 19th century as a kind of game-keeper's lookout. The church is mainly notable for a number of monuments to the Gage family who have occupied Firle Place from the 15th century to the present day.

Alciston is an interesting village which can be visited with only a slight detour from the described route. In medieval times Battle Abbey had estates here. Since then the village has shrunk a great deal but the fine and massive tithe barn remains as well as the ruins of a medieval dovecote.

Park in the village of West Firle which is reached by turning right (south) off the A27 Lewes-Eastbourne road about 5 miles east of Lewes. There is reasonable roadside parking near the village post office (OS map ref. 470072). Alternatively you can park at the top of Bo-peep Bostal (as for Walk 26) and start the walk there.

Start the walk along a stony track which leaves the village street in West Firle beside the post office and a telephone box. Notice the spring which rises to the left of the path and is enclosed by a stone wall with steps leading down to the water. The track leads you out into Firle Park through a swing gate. Now follow a clear track across parkland with Firle Place visible away to the right. Soon after crossing the access drive to Firle Place, veer slightly to the right across open parkland passing immediately to the left of a plantation and aiming for a tower which can be seen ahead on a low hill (the tower is obvious in winter but tends to be obscured by tree foliage in summer). Join a wide track through a bridle gate and turn right along it.

Ignore a track to the left and go ahead with a flint wall on your right. At a T-junction turn left. After a quarter of a mile, beside an interesting cottage with lancet windows, turn right. You are now on the old coach road which you should follow for nearly 2 miles along the foot of the Downs. In 1½ miles go straight over the metalled access road to the Downs at Bo-peep.

Bo-peep is marked on the first edition of the one-inch Ordnance Survey map as Bo-peep gate. It has been surmised that the curious name comes from the turnpike keeper's way of peeping out of his small window, but, in fact, the 18th century turnpike road, which superseded the old coach road, followed the line taken by the present A27.

After another ⅓ mile, soon after passing within sight of the Alciston tithe barn which can be seen, except in high summer, away through trees across a field to the left, you should turn right along the foot of a tree-lined bank. (To visit Alciston village, go straight on instead of turning right and almost immediately turn left. To rejoin the walk you must retrace your steps.)

After turning right along the foot of the bank, follow a path along the field edge at first. This leads gradually into a sunken enclosed track which climbs towards the Downs. This fine old track, locally reputed to have been an 18th century smugglers' route, was rescued from a state of total neglect and impassability a few years ago when it was cleared by volunteers belonging to the Sussex Rights of Way Group. It is now well used and is unlikely to become seriously obstructed again, but can be obscured by nettles in summer.

At the top of the sunken section of path, go over a stile and turn right on a wide grassy track which brings you out on the metalled bostal road. Climb with this to the top of the Downs and the South Downs Way where you should turn right. (From this point at the top of the bostal Walk 26 starts.)

Follow the South Downs Way to the top of Firle Beacon where the triangulation point is at a height of over 700 feet. About 200 yards beyond the summit, go through a bridle gate and after another 300 yards fork right on an unfenced path which soon runs along the top of the steepest part of the scarp slope. This will lead you to a clear terraced bridleway and you should follow this down to the foot of the hill. At the bottom, go through a bridle gate to the right of a wood and go along the left hand edge of a field with the wood on your left. Where the wood narrows after 250 yards go left for a few yards before turning right on a path within a line of trees. At a T-junction with a gate labelled 'Private' ahead, turn left on a wide track with a flint wall to the right and follow this back to the village of West Firle and the car.

HEIGHTON HILL AND BISHOPSTONE

WALK 26

★

7½ miles (12 km)

OS Landranger sheets 198 and 199

To the east of the River Ouse the Downs are at their narrowest — less than half a day's walk from the northern escarpment to the sea. This walk starts on the crest of the Downs at a height of 620 feet and drops down almost to sea level at Bishopstone, crossing a stretch of empty, rolling downland. There are not many landmarks but the tracks are clear and good except for one short stretch which is often obliterated by ploughing. It is difficult to believe that just beyond this unspoilt downland there is a belt of modern building development which has crept up almost to the village of Bishopstone.

Bishopstone is a typical downland village with a good deal of flintwork and a large and beautiful church, one of the finest in Sussex. Bishopstone was part of the see of Chichester from the 8th century onwards and much of the church dates back to that time. There is a Saxon sundial over the porch which still bears the name of Eadric, presumably the mason or donor, and the fine early Norman tower is prominently visible from the surrounding hills with the village, a huddle of roofs and trees, clustered round it.

Park in the car parking area on the top of the Downs at Bo-peep Bostal (a link point with Walk 25). To get there turn right (south) off the A27 Lewes-Eastbourne road about 7 miles east of Lewes, soon after passing the Barley Mow at Selmeston. The turning is at OS map ref. 507065. Follow the narrow bostal road for about 1½ miles to the top of the Downs where there is a parking area at OS map ref. 494050.

From the point where the tarmac road turns left at the top of the Downs to go to the car park, keep straight on through two gates, passing to the right of a Dutch barn, and continue in a south-westerly direction with a fence on your left. In half a mile, by a sheep fold, the track divides. Here, turn squarely right with a fence on your right. In 60 yards, go through a gateway into the next field and turn right, still with a fence, right. After another 220 yards, turn sharply left and begin to drop down along the field edge.

A clear path, well worn by horses' hooves, now unwinds ahead of you, down and then up again over Heighton Hill. Go through another bridle gate on the summit and keep along the right hand edge of the next field on high ground with gorse bushes to the right. At the end of this field, follow the fence line round to the left and, in 50 yards, go

To A27

Start

South Downs Way
(Walk 25)

Park Here

Dutch
Barn

N

Cattle Pen

Heighton Hill

Gardeners Hill

Water Pumping
Station

NORTON

Reservoir

Rookery
Hill

BISHOPSTONE

right over a stile to continue in a south-westerly direction, now with a
fence and gorse on the left, over the shoulder of Gardeners Hill with
the buildings of Newhaven in the distance ahead on the other side of
the Ouse valley.

Drop down into a dip and climb again straight ahead, ignoring two
tracks to the right. About two-thirds of the way up the other side, turn
left on a broad track which drops back down into the valley which you
then follow for nearly a mile. In just over ½ mile, after passing a water
pumping station on the right, the track becomes metalled.

Just before reaching the first house of the tiny hamlet of Norton,
turn right through a green-painted metal field gate and follow a clear
terraced track which curves to the left as it climbs to the top of the
hill.

From the top there are views of Newhaven harbour ahead and to the left can be seen the cliffs of Seaford Head at the western end of the Seven Sisters (see Walk 28).

At the top, after passing under power lines, turn left along the ridge of Rookery Hill with a fence line on your right. In little more than 100 yards, begin to bear left downhill on a faintly defined path, aiming towards Bishopstone church which can be seen ahead in the valley. Go through a gate and follow an enclosed path which drops downhill through a belt of woodland. At the bottom of the hill, just as the path levels out, go left over two stiles and along the edge of a field with a swampy area to the right and a flint wall on the left. After passing through a swing gate, go half right across an open field, aiming just to the left of the church. At the far corner of the field, go out through a gate and, almost immediately, turn right along a track. In 10 yards a path on the left is signposted across rough pasture to the churchyard and out to the road in Bishopstone village.

At the road turn left and in about 50 yards, after passing a barn on the right and just before the road drops down, turn right on a wide track which climbs uphill. Ignore the first track to the left and in another 150 yards, where the main track turns right, go left along a grassy path and over a stile to follow a splendid terraced grassy track along the side of the hill, with a hedged bank to the right and the hill sloping quite steeply down to the left. After passing through a bridle gate continue on a clear path with a fence on your right, soon passing a reservoir on the right. Follow this clear headland track, first with a hedge to your right and subsequently parallel and to the left of a concrete track, eventually joining a bridleway coming in from the right and following it past another reservoir. At a junction with a number of ways, keep straight ahead on the main track and follow it along the side of Denton Hill, passing the curiously named site of three barrows known as Five Lords Burgh (burgh comes from the Old English *beorg* meaning mound or tumulus). Keep on this clear track for 1½ miles before rejoining your outgoing route by the cattle pen. Retrace your steps to the car park.

Jevington
Holt

To Walk
30

SOUTH DOWNS WAY
(Unfenced)

The Long Man
of
Wilmington

Windover
Hill

Lullington
Heath
Nature
Reserve

WINCHESTER'S
POND

N ←

Reservoir

Lullington
Church

Plonk
Barn

Cuckmere
River

ALFRISTON

START

ALFRISTON AND LULLINGTON HEATH

WALK 27

★

5½ miles (9 km)

OS Landranger sheet 199

From Alfriston this walk crosses the Cuckmere river and then climbs steadily on to the Downs, passing near the tiny isolated church at Lullington, which lays claim to being the smallest church in England though it is really only part of the chancel of a larger structure.

The walk passes above the Long Man of Wilmington and then follows one of the finest stretches of the South Downs Way, unfenced across close cropped open pasture. The return route traverses Lullington Heath, a national nature reserve which conserves a rare mixture of chalk and heathland habitats.

The walk may be combined with Walk 30 (see text and sketch map) to provide a combined figure-of-eight circuit of 12½ miles.

Alfriston is an attractive village which, despite great tourist pressures, retains a strong flavour of its past. There is a tiny market place, with a tree and the stump of a market cross, and some fine old buildings, including the Star, a beautiful half-timbered inn with an overhanging upper storey, built in the early 15th century, probably as a rest house for pilgrims and mendicant friars travelling to and from Chichester. It has been carefully preserved, the carvings on the front of the building picked out in bright colours as they probably would have been centuries ago.

The lofty cruciform church is known as 'the cathedral of the Downs' and stands near the river on a mound, possibly of pagan religious origin. Nearby there is a pre-Reformation Clergy House, a humble place of timber and thatch, with a Sussex rammed chalk floor and a hall open to the sooty roof timbers. It was rescued from decay in 1896 and bought for £10 by the National Trust, the first building ever acquired by them, and is now open to the public.

Alfriston was a centre of the smuggling industry in the 18th century, Cuckmere Haven nearby being a good landing place. As many as a dozen cutters would anchor off the beach and be met by two or three hundred smugglers on horseback. Everybody was involved. If you heard horses' feet at midnight you didn't look out of the window, as Kipling's poem makes clear — 'Watch the wall, my darling, while the Gentlemen go by'.

Alfriston was also the centre of a sheep-shearing district in the days when flocks of sheep were to be seen everywhere on the Downs. As recently as 1932 the old folk custom of laying a tuft of wool on a shepherd's breast at his funeral was observed here — a gentle hint to the Almighty that shepherds have to work on Sunday and cannot always manage to go to church.

The Long Man of Wilmington, cut into the side of Windover Hill, is 226 feet high, the largest chalk figure in England. Theories abound as to his origins, but nothing is known for certain.

Park at Alfriston. There are two car parks in the village, a smaller one for which no charge is made, and a larger one nearby where parking will cost you 60 pence (at time of writing).

From the car parks make your way into the centre of the village. After passing the market cross, then the Star Inn on the right and the George Inn on the left, turn left along a narrow path between the houses which leads past the village green to a bridge over the Cuckmere river.

On the other side of the river, continue on a metalled path which crosses another footbridge to reach a lane opposite Plonk Barn. Turn right for 10 yards only, before going left through a swing gate and along a narrow path which climbs gently. Ignore a path to the left and continue to climb along a grassy headland.

After about 350 yards, a path back to the left leads to Lullington church, well worth a short detour. Return the same way and carry on for a few more yards to a lane where you should turn left.

After ¼ mile along the lane, just beyond a summit where a sudden view of the Weald opens out ahead, you should fork right, now back on the South Downs Way. A flint track climbs steadily up the shoulder of the hill. As you climb, pause to look back across Alfriston to a grand prospect of the Downs escarpment culminating in the distinctive profile of Firle Beacon (Walk 25).

The track passes to the right of a reservoir. After another 200 yards or so you have a choice. The South Downs Way forks right, round the back of Windover Hill. A much better route continues to climb along the edge of the scarp slope with a fence to the left. The path passes high above the head of the Long Man of Wilmington, not clearly visible from this viewpoint. The view over the Weald is immense, with the village of Wilmington tucked under the Downs and the waters of Arlington reservoir in the middle distance.

Beyond the next stile a little care is needed. Don't continue with the fence up to the top of the hill. Instead, bear half right for a few yards to rejoin the South Downs Way as it passes round the head of a combe. After 200 yards or so, fork left, still with the South Downs Way, which is now unfenced as it crosses a wide expanse of downland pasture, commanding a splendid view southwards towards Friston Forest and the sea. The route is marked by occasional wooden way posts with the familiar acorn logo.

After ¾ mile, you will come to a junction of paths where the South Downs Way turns left down the hill and provides a link with Walk 30. To continue with Walk 27, turn sharply back to the right here. The track soon runs within the boundary of the Lullington Heath Nature Reserve, descending into a dip and then climbing again.

Towards the top of the rise, seek out Winchester's Pond, hidden behind gorse to the right of the path. This is a restored dew pond, a haven for dragonflies and other pond insects.

At the top of the hill, go straight over a crossing track where the way ahead is signposted to Litlington. After almost $\frac{1}{2}$ mile, fork right, signposted to Lullington Court. A track now drops down steadily with Alfriston ahead of you in the valley.

Join a lane and turn sharply back to the left. After 200 yards, double back sharply to the right on a narrow path, part of the footpath alternative to the main South Downs Way. The path is enclosed at first, then beside a field. After a stile, cross a meadow and wind through scrub again, then, after another stile, continue beside a water meadow with a good view across the Cuckmere to Alfriston church and Clergy House. After another short path through scrub you will find yourself back on your outgoing route. Turn left over the river and back into Alfriston.

FRISTON FOREST AND THE SEVEN SISTERS

WALK 28

★

7 miles (11 km)

OS Landranger sheet 199

This is a walk within an area designated by the Countryside Commission as 'Heritage Coast'. It crosses a series of landscapes which are now protected from development and largely open for public access. The Cuckmere valley from Exceat Farm to the sea is part of the Seven Sisters Country Park, Friston Forest belongs to the Forestry Commission, Crowlink and the rest of the Seven Sisters are in the care of the National Trust.

The last team of black oxen in Sussex was ploughing at Exceat Farm in 1922. It is now the Park Centre of the Country Park. The conversion has preserved the farm buildings; an old barn shelters an exhibition and book stall and there is a café nearby.

The sheltered downland village of Westdean is almost surrounded by Friston Forest. Adjoining the church there is a 13th century parsonage, a solid flint house with narrow windows, originally without glass, which is thought to be one of the oldest inhabited houses in the country. It is possible that King Alfred had a manor house in the village. Charleston Manor, a mile to the north, is often open to the public and is well worth a visit.

Friston Forest is the only East Sussex equivalent of the many beech plantations on the West Sussex Downs. As you walk along the sheltered grassy rides, it is difficult to realize that the sea is so near. The forest is comparatively young, the trees still close together and fringed with nursery conifers.

The cliffs which make up the Seven Sisters must be nearly as famous as the white cliffs of Dover. They offer a most exhilarating walk which is rather strenuous because it involves crossing a succession of dry chalk valleys.

Walks 28 and 29 can be linked to give a combined length of 11½ miles. Alternatively, if you would like to include in your walk all of the Seven Sisters (instead of only 4½ of them), follow the described route of Walk 29 from the Crowlink car park as far as the cliff edge, where you can turn right and follow the cliffs along to rejoin the main walk. This will add about a mile to the total.

Park at the Seven Sisters Country Park car park at Exceat. Exceat is on the A259 Seaford to Eastbourne road about 2 miles east of Seaford, and the car park is to the south of the road about ¼ mile east of the road bridge over the River Cuckmere (OS map ref. 519995).

From the entrance to the car park, turn right along the A259 road for a few yards, passing the Country Park Centre on the left. Immediately beyond the centre, fork left on a roughly metalled track which leads you into a field. Climb straight up the grassy hillside and over a stile in a flint wall, passing a Forestry Commission notice and descending an elaborate flight of steps to the village of Westdean. At the bottom, keep straight on, ignoring turnings to right and left, and follow a narrow road round to the right, passing the church on your left. About 100 yards beyond the church, turn left at a T-junction.

The road, metalled at first, soon becomes a forestry track. Soon after passing a white-walled house on the left, fork left signposted to Jevington, still with the main track which soon becomes a wide forest ride and climbs. Ignore all side tracks and continue to ascend gently. Towards the top, views open out to the left — northwards to Windover Hill on the escarpment and westwards across the Cuckmere valley. After a full mile, turn right at a wide crossing track. There are no obviously describable features at this point, but the path to the left drops downhill and the one to the right (your route) climbs at first and is a wide grassy ride.

Follow the ride over a summit and downhill, ignoring side tracks. At the bottom of a valley, go over a forestry track and climb again through more mature beech forest, large areas of which have been clear felled. After leaving the afforested area, keep straight ahead on a grassy path over open downland and drop down to re-enter the forest. Go over a metalled drive and in 100 yards go ahead along another access driveway.

About 50 yards short of a car passing place on the drive, look out for a narrow path on the right which takes you through a swing gate into a large field. Go half left across this field on a path which can usually be seen trodden out, and go through another swing gate in the flint wall ahead. Cross a driveway and go over a stile into another large field. Go diagonally uphill across this field and over a stile in the far corner into woodland. Now follow a clear track out to the road at Friston pond and church.

Follow the 'No through road' to Crowlink which starts between pond and church. In 300 yards go past the National Trust parking area on the right. (This is the starting point for Walk 29 and also for the extended Seven Sisters walk described above.)

Go ahead across a cattle grid and almost immediately where the road veers right, down into the valley, go ahead to follow a track on high ground to the left of the Crowlink valley, traversing what must be one of the last remaining expanses of open permanent downland pasture in the entire South Downs. The buildings of Crowlink, nestling in the valley to your right, are now used as a holiday centre. On reaching the cliff edge you will find a sarsen stone commemorating the purchase of the Crowlink area in 1926 to provide public access and recreation.

Turn right along the cliff path and follow it over four of the Seven Sisters to the cliff above Cuckmere Haven. From here there are various routes back to the car park through the Seven Sisters Country Park. Here I will describe a good one.

Just as the cliff path begins to drop into the Cuckmere valley, turn right, with a fence on your left, on a path which keeps to higher ground along the side of the valley. After about half a mile where the main path curves to the left and drops down, continue along the hill side on an indistinct path, soon dropping steeply down into Foxhole Bottom, with its picturesque group of old farm buildings surrounded by sycamore trees. Keep round to the right of these buildings and then turn left and pass to the right of a modern barn. Go ahead through a bridle gate, and bear left over the shoulder of the hill, back to the car park.

FRISTON AND BELLE TOUT

WALK 29

★

4½ miles (7 km)

OS Landranger sheet 199

Another, shorter 'Heritage Coast' walk which can be linked with Walk 28 to provide a total circuit of 11½ miles. It traverses part of the National Trust Crowlink area, before dropping to Birling Gap and climbing again to the old Belle Tout lighthouse, built in 1831. The top, which housed the lantern, has now gone. The light was so often obscured by sea-fog that the lighthouse at the foot of Beachy Head was built to replace it in 1902. From the cliff top beyond Belle Tout there are good views of the newer lighthouse.

The return walk passes through Eastdean, which, like Alfriston, suffers from its popularity. The Tiger Inn, with its smuggling associations, and a group of flint and tile cottages surround the village green. The nearby church has an unusually wide flint tower which may have been built in this way to provide a refuge against raiders from the sea. Birling Gap offered a landing place not far away and was used centuries later by smugglers. Part of a row of coastguard cottages survive from the 19th century at Birling Gap, the rest having fallen into the sea, which is steadily eroding the whole length of chalk cliffs.

Friston lost its windmill years ago, but its characteristic downland church remains exposed to the winds on the top of the hill, with the old village pond nearby. Much of the church is Saxon and it has an open timber roof dated about 1450. Little of the original village remains, but a new village has spread fairly unobtrusively down the hillside, merging with a similar development north of Eastdean.

Park at the National Trust car parking area at Crowlink. Turn south off the A259 Seaford to Eastbourne road at Friston, about 4 miles east of Seaford. The turning is a 'No Through Road' which starts between Friston pond and church almost opposite the B2105 turn-off. The car parking area is on the right in about 300 yards at OS map ref. 550979.

To start the walk go back along the track by which you reached the car park for 75 yards before going right through a field gate. Go diagonally to the right across open pasture aiming for a swing gate which can be seen in the fence ahead. Immediately beyond the gate turn left and walk parallel to and a little way away from the fence line on your left. Go through a bridle gate ahead and on through a narrow belt of trees. Now take a well trodden path along the left hand edge of pasture with woodland dropping away to the left, heading for a barn with a red roof. After passing to the right of the barn, follow a path along the crest of Went Hill, eventually dropping down to the left of the ridge as you approach the cliff edge. Where the main track curves to the left, keep straight on through a bridle gate. After a second bridle gate, pass to the right of a group of houses and then turn left and follow a wide track down to Birling Gap.

Take a narrow path which starts from the road at Birling Gap to the left of a telephone box. Climb up on to the cliffs and follow the cliff edge path past a coastguard lookout and on for ½ mile to the disused Belle Tout lighthouse. From the top there is a fine view back along the line of the Seven Sisters to Seaford Head. Keep to the left of the lighthouse buildings, and, as you continue along the cliff edge, the newer lighthouse comes into view at the foot of Beachy Head.

On reaching a road at a sharp bend, turn left and follow a grassy track which runs parallel and to the left of the road. In a little under ¼ mile, turn right and drop to the road on a grassy track. Go straight across the road and through a metal gate to follow a wide track, fenced on the left. In just under ½ mile, where the main track curves to the right, go straight on, soon crossing a driveway through two bridle gates and continue on a clear track, eventually with a flint wall to your left. After going through a bridle gate, turn left, keeping a wall and then a copse on your left. Pass to the right of the first of the buildings of Birling Farm and make your way out via two bridle gates and an access drive to a road.

Turn right along the road and follow it to the village of Eastdean; luckily there is a fairly wide grass verge. At the edge of the village fork left, signposted Eastdean village, and follow this road past the church on the right. On reaching the village green with a shop and the Tiger Inn beside it, turn sharply left along Went Way. In about 100 yards, turn right up some steps and climb on a narrow path with a flint wall to the right. This leads you out on to a sloping grassy hillside. Keep straight ahead uphill with a flint wall a little way away to the right. In 150 yards or so, turn right over the wall using some stone steps. Keep to the left of another wall which goes away at a right angle on the other side, and follow the right hand edge of pasture — you are now back on National Trust land. Where the fence on your right turns away to the right, keep straight ahead across open pasture and so back to the car park which you can see ahead.

The car park at the start and finish of this walk is the link point with Walk 28.

FOLKINGTON

Park Here

Start

Ch

WALK 30

B2105
To Polegate

WANNOCK

B2105
To Jevington

WILLINGDON

N

Combe Hill

Babylon Down

To
Walk
27

B2105
To Polegate

Ch

Willingdon Bottom

JEVINGTON

B2105
To Friston

FOLKINGTON AND JEVINGTON

WALK 30

★

6 miles (9.5 km)

OS Landranger sheet 199

There is something very pleasing about the approach by road to the tiny village of Folkington (pronounced Fohwington), turning off the busy A27 along a quiet lane with leads to the foot of the Downs and comes to an abrupt end by the beautiful church among the trees.

From Folkington, the walk follows the old road along the foothills to Jevington, surely one of the most picturesque of all downland villages, half hidden by trees as you come down to it from the hill.

From Jevington the walk becomes very characteristic of the bare East Sussex downland, especially the gentle climb to the top of Babylon Down with its wide views over the Weald and the spread of Eastbourne towards Pevensey Levels.

This walk may be conveniently linked with Walk 27, giving a total distance of 12½ miles.

Park at Folkington church. Turn left (south) off the A27 Eastbourne-Lewes road about a mile east of Polegate on to a narrow cul-de-sac road to Folkington. Park where the metalled road ends, just beyond Folkington church at OS map ref. 559038.

Start the walk by taking the left fork where the metalled road ends beyond Folkington church, dropping slightly downhill on a wide track which subsequently climbs and winds through the downland foothills for 1½ miles. Finally, at a T-junction with a wide chalky track, turn right and climb. In about 150 yards, fork left and follow the main track which soon becomes a sunken path between banks. In ¼ mile, fork left and in 50 yards you will come to a T-junction. To link with Walk 27, turn right here and climb with the South Downs Way for ¼ mile to the link point at OS map ref. 553019. To continue with Walk 30, turn left at this T-junction, following the South Downs Way in the other direction, downhill through woodland, then with a field on your right to pass Jevington church and exit on to a road. Turn right for 15 yards before going left along Willingdon Lane. Where the lane ends keep straight ahead on a grassy track. In 150 yards fork left on the (slightly) higher of two tracks. After going through a field gate this becomes a well trodden path through scrub. Go on through a bridle gate and follow a wide track along the floor of Willingdon Bottom.

The left hand slope of this dry valley is marked on the map as a field system, rising towards the crest of Combe Hill, where there are traces of a Neolithic causewayed camp. Although the hillside is partly obscured by scrub, many of the lynchets can be seen, looking like great steps in the grass.

Where the valley divides into two, go ahead through another bridle gate and climb out of the valley with a fence on your right on to the top of Babylon Down. On reaching a car parking area turn left and follow the ridge of the downland with extensive views across Willingdon and Eastbourne to the sea. At a point in a dip where a number of paths converge, bear slightly right and take a path which drops down round the left hand edge of a combe, passing a wooden seat. Where the path forks half way down the hill, bear left round the shoulder. On reaching a belt of woodland, turn sharply right, dropping down along the edge of the wooded area. Fairly soon, go left through a swing gate and continue to descend with the wood on your left. In about 150 yards, turn left at a crossing track along a grassy headland path with a small cemetery to the right. Follow this stiled path, running parallel to the back gardens of houses, through two fields and on along an enclosed track beside allotments and out to the road at Wannock.

Turn left along the road and, after 150 yards, about 50 yards beyond the entrance to a house called 'Broadwater', turn right through a gate and along a narrow path which crosses a bridge over the end of a pond, skirts to the left of a garden and comes out on an estate road where you should turn left. At the end of this cul-de-sac, go ahead over a stile and immediately turn right. In a few yards only, bear left on a clear path, across an open field at first then veering left to pick up a hedge on your left near the far left field corner. In the field corner, go over two stiles and cross another field towards a line of trees on the skyline. On reaching the trees, go over a concrete track and another stile and follow a narrow path through a belt of woodland. Cross a stile into a field and bear half left across it to a stile which takes you out into a road. Turn left on the road and follow it for a little over $\frac{1}{4}$ mile back to Folkington and the car.